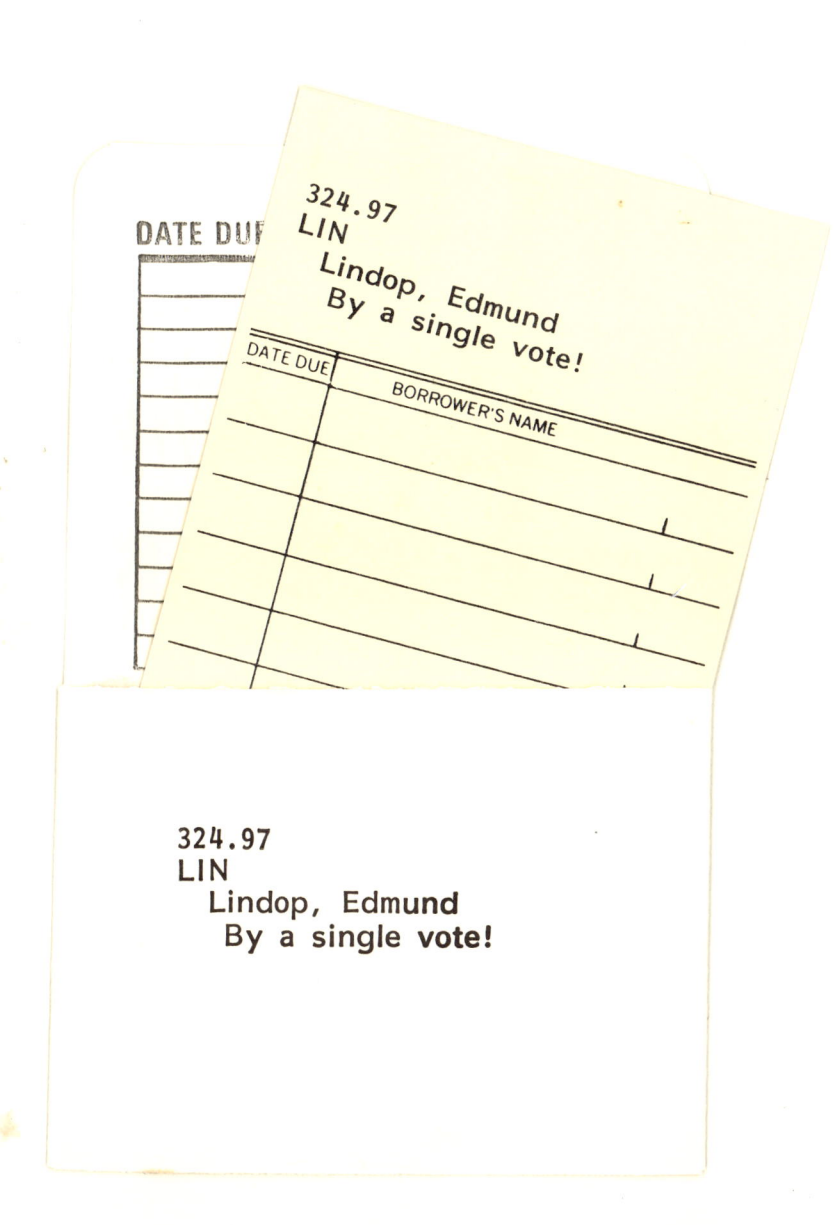

BY A SINGLE VOTE!

324.97
LIN
Lindop, Edmund
By a single vote!

324.97
LIN
Lindop, Edmund
By a single vote!

BY A SINGLE VOTE!

One-Vote Decisions That Changed American History

Edmund Lindop

Stackpole Books

Copyright ©1987 by Edmund Lindop

Published by *90-147*
STACKPOLE BOOKS
Cameron and Kelker Streets
P.O. Box 1831
Harrisburg, PA 17105

All rights reserved, including the right to reproduce this book or portions thereof in any form or by any means, electronic or mechanical, including photocopying, recording, or by any information storage and retrieval system, without permission in writing from the publisher. All inquiries should be addressed to Stackpole Books, Cameron and Kelker Streets, P.O. Box 1831, Harrisburg, Pennsylvania 17105.

Printed in the United States of America

10 9 8 7 6 5 4 3 2 1

Library of Congress Cataloging-in-Publication Data

Lindop, Edmund.
    By a single vote!

    Bibliography: p.
    Includes index.
    1. Elections—United States—History. 2. Voting—United States—History. I. Title.
JK1965.L56   1987   324.973   87-1936
ISBN 0-8117-2090-X

Contents

Acknowledgments	7
Preface	9
The Fate of a Nation Hangs in the Balance	11
Can the Senate Prevent the President from Firing His Appointees?	14
The Chief Justice Is Burned in Effigy	15
A Tie-Breaking Vote Leads to a Stabbing	21
A Nonconformist in the Electoral College	24
God and Stephen Van Rensselaer	25
Calhoun Breaks a Tie and Reaps the "Tariff of Abominations"	30
"Kill Him, Sir, Kill Him Dead"	32
The Only Vice President Elected by the Senate	37
A Vice President Helps Polk Keep His Pledge	40
A Whiff of Glory	43
A President Stands Trial	43
Limiting the Scope of the Fourteenth Amendment	54
President by a Single Vote	56
A Court Decision Leads to the Sixteenth Amendment	66
You Can Unscramble Eggs	68

Reforming the Election of Senators	*70*
Women Fight for the Ballot	*73*
The Invisible Empire Escapes Condemnation	*78*
The Vice President Is Asleep at the Switch	*81*
The Newspaper That Would Not Stay Gagged	*83*
A Stitch in Time Saves Nine	*86*
A Narrow Escape from National Peril	*89*
Trying to Reduce the President's Powers	*92*
The Rights of the Accused	*96*
A Second Constitutional Convention?	*99*
Lowering the Voting Age	*102*
The Court Zigzags on Capital Punishment	*106*
What Is Obscenity?	*109*
Affirmative Action and Reverse Discrimination	*112*
A Judicial Appointment in Jeopardy	*115*
Major 5-4 Supreme Court Decisions in 1985–1986	*117*
Epilogue	*122*
Further Reading	*123*
Index	*125*

Acknowledgments

The author expresses his gratitude to Joy Crane Thornton and Kevin Berntson for reading the manuscript and making valuable suggestions.

Preface

On a spring day in 1985 the voters in Andover, Massachusetts, held their annual town meeting. One disputed issue was whether to permit a company to install a parking lot on public land. Those in favor of the measure argued that the lot would provide needed parking; opponents claimed that allowing private use of public land was unwise and would set a bad precedent.

When the election was held, people stood up to be counted. The results were announced: 257 voted yes on the parking lot, 256 voted no. Nineteen persons in the room had not voted on this measure that carried by one lone vote.

Because of the razor-thin margin, opponents of the parking lot asked for a second election. Meanwhile, two persons in the back of the room who had abstained asked a man why he had voted against the measure. People in other parts of the hall also were conferring about the issue.

A second vote was taken, and this time everyone rose to be counted. The decision was reversed; by a count of 271 to 261, the citizens turned down the parking lot. The two persons in the back of the room who had abstained before now joined those who voted against the measure.

The parking lot issue was decided by only a small fraction of Andover's registered voters. Unfortunately, this same lack of participation in elections is repeated again and again across the entire United States. Our nation usually records lower voter turnouts than any of the world's other democracies. Even in presidential elections, with all the publicity generated by the media, voter participation is shockingly low. In 1984, only about 53 percent of the total adult population cast ballots to determine who would hold the highest office in the land. And in most state and local elections the percentage of voters drops much lower.

No one can be absolutely certain about the outcome of an election before the votes are cast and counted. The voters who stay away from the polls may determine, by their inaction, the success or failure of a ballot measure or a candidate running for office.

Elections may be won by huge landslides, by comfortable majorities and pluralities, or by narrow margins. This book tells about some of the closest of all elections—those that were won or lost by a single vote. At the time they occurred, these one-vote decisions profoundly influenced current events, and some of them helped shape the course of history for years to come.

Democratic elections have been described as the magic of numbers. Sometimes the essence of this magic is distilled into one precious vote.

The Fate of a Nation Hangs in the Balance

An ominous question loomed like a huge dark cloud over the Constitutional Convention that met at Philadelphia in the summer of 1787. Were the states to be represented in the new national legislature equally or in proportion to their populations?

Delegates from states with large populations, such as Virginia, Massachusetts, and Pennsylvania, argued that representation in Congress should be based entirely on population. They claimed that if one state had ten times as many people as another state, it should have ten times as many representatives in Congress. "Can we forget for whom we are forming a government?" asked James Wilson of Pennsylvania. "Is it for *men*, or for the imaginary beings called *states*?"

But the delegates from the small states were not swayed by this argument. They insisted that every state must have equal representation in the new Congress. Each state had one vote in the Articles of Confederation Congress that was then governing the nation, and this principle should be continued in the new government. Otherwise, the small states would always be subservient to the will of their larger neighbors. "I will never accede to a plan," thundered Luther Martin of Maryland, "that will introduce an inequality and lay ten states at the mercy of Virginia, Massachusetts, and Pennsylvania."

The delegates from states with small populations were prepared to break up the convention and leave for home if they did not get their way. Delaware's John Dickinson asserted that "we would rather submit to a foreign power than submit to be deprived of an equality of suffrage in both branches of the Legislature, and thereby be thrown under the domination of the large states."

12 / *By a Single Vote!*

William Paterson of New Jersey echoed this sentiment, claiming that his state would "never confederate" if it did not have an equal voice in Congress, because it "would be swallowed up" by the larger states. And Gunning Bedford, Jr., of Delaware warned that his tiny state might do even more than withdraw from the Union — it might seek an alliance with some European country!

Delegates from the large states stubbornly held their ground, and some hinted that military action might be needed to solve the problem. Pennsylvania's Gouverneur Morris, conscious of the greater wealth, resources and manpower of the larger states, bluntly declared, "This country must be united. If persuasion does not unite, the sword will."

This issue of representation in Congress — fraught with rising tension that neared the breaking point — gravely threatened the work of the convention and the entire future of the United States. Benjamin Franklin, the oldest convention delegate and one of the wisest, was so perplexed by this angry dispute that he suggested a chaplain be hired to open each session with prayer. But the convention had no funds to pay a chaplain, and delegate Alexander Hamilton was said to have remarked that no "foreign aid" was needed.

Franklin, the patient peacemaker, urged the warring delegates to seek a compromise. Alluding to the work of a carpenter, he said, "When a broad table is to be made, and the edges of the planks do not fit, the artist takes a little from both sides and makes a good joint. In like manner both sides must part with some of their demands, in order that they may join in some accommodating proposition."

Roger Sherman of Connecticut suggested such a compromise: Let representation in one house of Congress be based on population and representation in the other house be equal for all the states. On July 2, 1787, a motion was made to allow each state an equal voice in the upper house, or Senate. The vote was a tie. Five states voted yes; five states voted no. (The Georgia delegation voted evenly, so the state could not cast its ballot. The New Hampshire delegates had not yet arrived at Philadelphia, and Rhode Island had refused to send any representatives to the convention.)

Following the tie vote, neither side would budge; the delegates were caught in the grip of a stagnating deadlock. Roger Sherman sadly observed that the convention had come to a "full stop." If this impasse had continued, there would have been no Constitution, no strong central government, no United States as we know it today. The earnest, hard working men at Philadelphia would have bungled their glorious opportunity to forge a proud and powerful new nation. They would have returned

The Fate of a Nation Hangs in the Balance / 13

to their homes, still saddled with the hopelessly weak Articles of Confederation government they had sought to replace.

No more crucial situation ever confronted a group of Americans than this paralyzing stalemate at the Constitutional Convention. As Gouverneur Morris later admitted, "The fate of America was suspended by a hair."

Some dejected delegates virtually gave up hope of breaking the deadlock, but others clung to the belief that there must be some way to surmount the obstacle that prevented the convention from moving ahead. Charles Cotesworth Pinckney of South Carolina was one of these optimists. He proposed the appointment of a Grand Committee, consisting of one member from each state, to devise some reasonable compromise on the question of representation in Congress. In desperation, the convention grasped at this suggestion, and the committee members were selected.

On July 5 the Grand Committee presented a compromise plan to the convention. It was much like the compromise suggested earlier by Roger Sherman, which the convention had rejected. In the House of Representatives each state would be allowed one representative for every forty thousand (later changed to thirty thousand) of its inhabitants. In the Senate each state would be allowed the same number of senators. Then the Grand Committee added a third point that was not included in Sherman's original proposal. The House of Representatives would have the sole power to originate money bills. This was a major concession to the large states, since they would dominate the House of Representatives and thus control the nation's purse strings.

Eleven more days were filled with debate about this compromise measure, which still did not satisfy the most contentious delegates. Finally, on July 16, the vote was taken. Five states voted for the compromise: Connecticut, Delaware, New Jersey, Maryland, and North Carolina. Four states voted against it: Pennsylvania, Virginia, South Carolina, and Georgia. Massachusetts was divided, the New Hampshire delegation still had not arrived, and New York could not vote because two of its three delegates had gone home, thus robbing the state of a quorum.

Other problems had to be solved before the Constitution was completed and approved by the delegates. But the thorniest question—the one that threatened to wreck the convention—had been resolved by a 5-4 vote of the states. By a single vote the logjam had been broken, and the Founding Fathers could then proceed with the task of constructing the framework for a mighty nation.

14 / By a Single Vote!

Can the Senate Prevent the President from Firing His Appointees?

The sole constitutional power of the vice president is to preside over the Senate and cast the tie-breaking vote if the senators are evenly divided on a bill. The first recorded vote by a vice president was cast by John Adams on July 18, 1789.

The question under consideration in both houses of Congress was whether the Senate had to concur if the president wanted to remove from office a person he had previously appointed. Under the Constitution it was clear that the president could make certain appointments only with the advice and consent of the Senate (expressed by a majority vote of the Senate). But the Constitution said nothing about whether the president needed the approval of the Senate to dismiss these officers.

Some members of Congress greatly feared executive power. Though they trusted George Washington, they were concerned that some future president might recklessly abuse his power and get rid of honest, competent officials who disagreed with him. To protect against this happening, they felt the Senate should decide if the president could fire the officials he had originally hired.

Other congressmen and senators came to the defense of the chief executive. Representative James Madison of Virginia claimed that if the Founding Fathers (of whom he was one) had intended to give this power to the Senate, they would have expressly included it in the Constitution. But since they did not do this, the right of removal was part of the general grant of power to the executive under Article II of the Constitution, which Congress could not reduce or change. Moreover, Madison argued, the president had the responsibility for the administration of the executive branch, and if he could not dismiss the head of a department without the Senate's approval, the president would be "no longer answerable" for what might occur in the branch of the government he headed.

When the issue came to a vote in the Senate, the count was 10 to 10. Vice President Adams opposed the measure that would have weakened the president's power, and he proudly voted against it. Actually, his vote was not needed to kill the measure because any question on which the Senate is evenly divided automatically is defeated unless the vice president casts an affirmative vote. But if a single senator had switched his vote, the measure would have passed by an 11-9 margin.

Ironically, this same issue recurred in 1867 to haunt the man who was then president, Andrew Johnson. Congress passed the Tenure of Office

Act by which the president was forbidden to remove appointed officials without the Senate's approval. When Johnson broke this act and subsequently stood trial for impeachment (see pages 51–54), the same arguments were used against him that had first been raised in 1789. The Supreme Court in 1926 finally struck down as unconstitutional the Senate's power to rule on presidential dismissals, thus reaffirming the decision made in Washington's administration.

Incidentally, John Adams frequently voted to break ties in the Senate. He cast ballots on twenty-nine measures, which still is the record number of votes for any vice president.

The Chief Justice Is Burned in Effigy

In 1794 the United States was on the brink of another war with Great Britain. The British refused to surrender their posts in the Old Northwest eleven full years after they had promised to give them up. British fur traders in this region continued to reap rich profits that rightfully belonged to Americans.

Furthermore, the British were extending their influence over the Indian tribes in the Old Northwest. They were using the Indians to hold back the steadily advancing American frontiersmen. Assuring the Indians that the Union Jack soon would fly again over the entire region north and west of the Ohio River, British agents supplied the tribes with muskets, ammunition, and scalping knives. The slaughter of American pioneers on the Ohio frontier with arms that bore British trademarks continued unabated.

Americans thus were thwarted from pushing westward to settle and develop lands ceded to them by the Peace Treaty of 1783. This injustice would persist as long as the British held onto the posts in the Northwest. The gravity of this situation troubled President George Washington, who said in August 1794: "I will undertake, without the gift of prophecy, to predict that it will be impossible to keep this country in a state of amity with Great Britain long, if the posts are not surrendered."

The fur posts and marauding Indians were not the only sources of strife between the United States and Great Britain in 1794. The British also pursued naval policies that struck heavily at American shipping. Britain was then at war with France and had no intention of respecting American neutrality on the seas. British warships seized scores of American vessels, mostly in the West Indies, confiscated their cargoes as contraband, and threw their crews into foul dungeons. At a single Caribbean port 130 American ships were captured as war prizes. When the British stormed the French island of Martinique in February 1794, they took all the American vessels in the harbor and locked up their 250 sailors on a prison ship. Farther out on the Atlantic Ocean the British forcibly boarded United States ships, stripped them of cargoes they claimed were headed for French ports, and often impressed (kidnapped) American sailors, charging that they were deserters from the British navy.

Britain was not the only warring country to harass American shipping. The warships and privateers of France and also of Spain and Holland (two of Britain's allies) frequently preyed on vessels that flew the American flag.

But it was the British offenses that ignited the wrath of the American public. Wounds had not yet healed from the recent war in which the British had inflicted death and suffering on thousands of Americans who had dared to fight for their independence. And now John Bull was vengefully wreaking havoc on United States shipping, arrogantly disregarding the trading rights of a neutral country, and effectively preventing the expansion of Americans into their own Northwest.

Southern plantation owners had another longstanding quarrel with the British. During the Revolutionary War British armies had carried away thousands of slaves, and after the war the British government turned a deaf ear to the Southerners' demands for compensation.

Moreover, at this time there was widespread sympathy in America for France in its war with Great Britain. The French had been our invaluable allies in the Revolutionary War, and without their enormous financial and military aid it is doubtful the Americans could have achieved their independence. Also, France was in the midst of a titanic revolution; its people, like ours, had shed the rule of an oppressive king. The French creed of "liberty, equality, and fraternity" impressed many Americans as a glorious corollary to "life, liberty, and the pursuit of happiness."

So, for various reasons, the clamor for war against Great Britain was once again heard throughout the land. At Marblehead, Massachusetts, three thousand resurgent "minutemen" drilled on the common, while two hundred sailors at nearby Gloucester rushed to the town fort and proclaimed they would protect it against any British invaders. Congress passed a bill authorizing funds to repair all seacoast harbors. Citizens in New York, including grocers, bakers, and college students, volunteered their services to help build fortifications. Congress also appropriated money to begin a navy, starting with six warships.

In March 1794, Congress imposed a thirty-day embargo on all American trading vessels bound for foreign ports. Although this order halted trade to France, it was obviously aimed mainly at Britain, and the American public accepted it enthusiastically. When the embargo failed to produce any concessions from Britain, Congress extended it for another month.

Then the embargo expired, and a renewed rash of hostility toward Britain broke out. An infuriated mob in Charleston, South Carolina, tore down the statue of William Pitt (Lord Chatham), the great British statesman whom American colonists had honored for his important part in winning the French and Indian War. In New York when John Hodgkinson, a popular actor, appeared on stage in the uniform of a British officer, as his role required, he was subjected to such violent catcalls and hisses that he had to stop the performance and explain to the audience that he was playing the part of a bully and coward. Angry Philadelphia citizens assaulted the front of Christ Church and tore from its facade the bas-relief of George II, who ruled England when the church had been built.

Political parties were just beginning in the United States, and the Republicans (also called Democratic-Republicans) fanned the growing resentment toward Great Britain. Led by Thomas Jefferson and James Madison, the Republicans formed clubs and societies that were virulently anti-British. The other early political party, the Federalists, drew much of its support from the maritime and mercantile groups in New England and the middle states, who generally were pro-British because of their close business ties with British merchants. Alexander Hamilton, the chief Federalist leader, was an unabashed Anglophile. President Washington distrusted political parties and tried to avoid their conflicts, but on most major issues he sided with the Federalists.

As the war fever continued to escalate, the president and his Federalist advisers grew very concerned. War with Great Britain, while perhaps justified, could spell disaster for the United States. Our country was virtually defenseless, with no standing army and only a handful of warships still on the drawing boards. Moreover, war with Britain could easily lead to the total collapse of the economy. The financial structure of the United States, fashioned expertly by Treasury Secretary Hamilton, depended heavily on customs duties, and about ninety percent of America's imports came from Britain. To cut off this major source of income and at the same time spend huge sums to wage a war could cause financial chaos and shake the very foundations of the Union.

So, in desperation, President Washington was willing to take any reasonable action that might avert a war many felt was inevitable. When he learned that Britain was modifying some of its most onerous naval policies, the president interpreted this as a hopeful sign. He decided that this was the time to send a special envoy to London to try to reconcile some of the differences between the two countries.

The man selected for this delicate mission was John Jay, chief justice of the Supreme Court. Because he was a Federalist known to have pro-British leanings, the Republicans in the Senate argued against Jay's appointment for three days. But his nomination was finally confirmed on April 19, 1794, and Jay sailed for England to pursue one of the most difficult tasks ever entrusted to a statesman.

Meanwhile, the Republicans in Congress were intent on resuming the trade embargo against Britain. Favoring a policy that would not affect trade with France and other countries, they introduced a bill to stop all trade with Britain. This bill alarmed President Washington and the Federalists, who did not want to cut off the badly needed revenue from British trade. Nor did they want to offend Britain while Jay's crucial negotiations were under way.

Nevertheless, the controversial bill passed in the House, where membership was closely divided between Republicans and Federalists. And it came dangerously close to passing in the Senate, even though the Federalists clearly controlled the upper house. The vote in the Senate was tied, and Vice President John Adams cast his tie-breaking vote with those who opposed the measure.

The prospects for the success of Jay's mission were not favorable. Before Jay left for England, Hamilton had told the chief justice that the British held most of the high cards. America's only high card was the threat that if reasonable terms were not obtained, the United States might join Sweden and Denmark in a newly formed armed neutrality pact to guarantee freedom of the seas to neutral countries. But Hamilton privately informed George Hammond, the British minister in Philadelphia, that the United States under no circumstances would join the new league of armed neutrality. So, in effect, Hamilton trumped his own nation's lone high card, turning the United States into a supplicant rather than a negotiator.

After months of discussion, Jay and Britain's Lord Grenville finally signed a "treaty of amity, commerce, and navigation" on November 19,

1794. By its terms the British promised to surrender the posts in the Northwest by June 1796, which was a major concession. The British also promised to open their West Indies to a small amount of American trade and to refer the claims against them for the destruction of American shipping to a mixed commission for arbitration.

The United States, on the other hand, guaranteed the payment of debts owed to the British before the Revolutionary War and agreed that the exact amount would be decided by another mixed commission. Furthermore, the United States pledged that it would not export certain products, such as cotton and sugar, in American vessels. This was an unfortunate concession, since Eli Whitney had invented the cotton gin the year before the treaty was signed, and Southerners looked forward to profiting from a huge cotton industry.

Under the Jay Treaty the British adamantly refused to give the United States the right as a neutral nation to trade openly with France. On several other matters of importance to Americans, the treaty was silent. It said nothing about the British practice of impressing American sailors, an emotional issue that had aroused great indignation throughout the United States. Also, the treaty said nothing about compensation for the black slaves the British had carried away, nor did it promise that the British would quit tampering with the Indians along the frontier.

Jay himself had no illusions that his treaty satisfied all the American demands, but he defended it as the best that could be obtained under the circumstances. When a copy of the treaty finally reached President Washington nearly four months after it was negotiated, he, too, was disappointed with its contents. But the president was faced with a difficult choice: either accept the treaty or, almost certainly, see the country plunged into a war it was ill-prepared to fight.

Washington wanted to avoid war at all costs while the United States was still weak and torn by dissension between anti-British Republicans who clamored for retribution and pro-British Federalists who opposed a conflict with America's best trading partner. The day would come, Washington believed, when the United States would be powerful enough to command respect and defend its interests from a position of strength — but that was not the situation in 1795.

Fearful of the storm of criticism that the treaty would arouse, Washington kept its terms secret, and so did the Senate when it began to debate the treaty on June 8. For sixteen grueling days Federalists and Republicans fiercely argued the merits of the first major treaty to come before the Senate for its "advice and consent," as required in the Constitution. The president wanted the senators to ratify the document, but he shrewdly agreed when they deleted the provision forbidding the United States to export cotton and other products in American ships because this was too degrading even for the Federalists to accept.

The ratification of a treaty requires a two-thirds vote of the Senate. When the Jay Treaty came up for ratification on June 24, 1795, its supporters and opponents knew that the vote would be very close. It carried by a vote of 20 to 10, exactly the two-thirds margin needed for ratification. All eighteen Federalist senators, one independent, and one lone Republican senator approved the measure. If any of these senators had defected, one of the most important treaties in our nation's history would have been rejected by a single vote!

The president and the Senate wanted to keep the treaty shrouded in secrecy until after the British government also had ratified it, but a Republican senator leaked its terms to a Philadelphia newspaper. Once the story was printed, resentment swept the country like a tornado. Flags were lowered to half-mast, bonfires were started with copies of the treaty, and protest meetings were held to condemn the document that "betrayed America." When Hamilton attempted to speak in New York, he was pelted with stones and forced from the platform, bleeding at the mouth. In Boston groups of rabid Republicans roamed the streets, breaking the windows of known supporters of the treaty. Irate mobs in Philadelphia so frightened John Adams that he feared they would overthrow the government. When a Kentucky senator who had voted for the treaty went home, he was beaten by a frenzied crowd and nearly drowned in a pond.

Even President Washington, the most beloved figure of his time, did not escape severe criticism for supporting the Jay Treaty. He was denounced as a tyrant, a hypocrite, a doddering old fool. His own former secretary of state, Thomas Jefferson, in an uncontrolled burst of fury said of the first president, "Curse on his virtues; they have undone the country." Then he accused Washington of being in the company of those "who had their heads shorn by the harlot England."

But the most scathing attacks were spewed forth on the Supreme Court chief justice who had put his name to the treaty. From Vermont to Georgia John Jay was condemned as a traitor who had sold his country down the river. Scores of towns were lighted at night by burning effigies of "that damned arch-traitor, Sir John Jay." In Charleston another effigy of Jay was hauled about in a dung cart and then hanged. On a fence in Massachusetts this irrational message was painted: "Damn John Jay! Damn everyone that won't damn John Jay! Damn everyone that won't put lights in his windows and sit up all night damning John Jay!" Even the French joined in the tumultuous derision of the chief justice with a sarcastic toast that was drunk to "the Republic of America. May she never mistake Jaybirds for eagles."

John Jay was unquestionably the nation's most hated man. It was said that he could walk at night from one end of the country to the other and find his way by the light of fires burning him in effigy.

Yet most historians believe that the treaty for which Jay was ruthlessly shamed, imperfect as it was, brought some enormously significant benefits to the infant United States. It forced the British to relinquish the posts in the Northwest and allowed Americans to develop that rich part of their country. It enhanced the stature of the United States as a nation that could meet on equal terms with Great Britain and hammer out an agreement that settled some of their differences. Probably most important, the Jay Treaty helped avoid an imminent war with the British.

To be sure, seventeen years later the United States did go to war with John Bull. But the Jay Treaty gave young Jonathan (as the British called the United States) precious time to grow, to become stronger, wealthier, and more populous, so that when the War of 1812 erupted, young Jonathan could hold his own against John Bull.

So the Jay Treaty may well have saved the United States in an hour of dark peril. What would have happened if a single senator who voted to ratify the treaty changed his mind and cast the additional no vote that would have killed the treaty? Would the United States soon have been at war with Britain? If so, would our nation have survived?

A Tie-Breaking Vote Leads to a Stabbing

On March 1, 1796, President Washington made his long-delayed announcement that the Jay Treaty, duly signed and ratified, was now the law of the land. But this much-maligned treaty was forced to face still another tough battle. In order to put it into effect, about $90,000 had to be appropriated. And the Constitution decrees that all money bills must originate in the House of Representatives.

Republicans in the House were determined to scuttle the Jay Treaty by withholding the appropriations needed to make it effective. The day after President Washington announced that the treaty had been approved, Representative Edward Livingston introduced a motion calling for the president to lay before the House the instructions that had been given to Jay and all other correspondence related to the treaty.

This motion unleashed a constitutional tempest in the House. Federalist congressmen insisted that the president and the Senate have the full power to make and ratify treaties without any interference from the House. Republican congressmen had a different opinion. Representative Albert Gallatin claimed that since the Constitution gives the House the right to originate all money bills, if a treaty requires an appropriation, then the House has a veto power over that treaty. Representative James Madison agreed, maintaining that the House is not a mere instrument of the president and must act in a responsible manner whenever it performs one of its functions, in this case making an appropriation.

For two weeks the House engaged in acrimonious debate and finally voted 62 to 37 to demand the treaty papers from the president. But Washington refused to submit these papers, implying that they were none of the House's business. In his reply to the House, the president referred to the larger question of who had the power to make and ratify treaties. "It is perfectly clear to my understanding," Washington wrote, "that the assent of the House of Representatives is not necessary to the validity of [a] treaty."

The president's stubborn refusal to comply with the House's request did not lessen the Republicans' resolve to strangle the Jay Treaty. After counting noses, they figured that the appropriation measure would go down to defeat by about six votes. But some of the most persuasive Federalists, joined by prominent businessmen, exerted strong pressure on the Republicans to accept the treaty for the good of the nation. They argued that while the fate of the treaty was uncertain, commerce languished. Ships remained at their docks, farm prices declined, and the value of stocks slid lower and lower. After listening to these arguments, some of the House Republicans, particularly those from northern states, began to waver.

Then, on April 28, Federalist Congressman Fisher Ames delivered one of the most impassioned speeches ever heard in the House. Ailing and fearful that he soon would die, Ames summoned all his strength to warn his colleagues that if the treaty were rejected, war would break out and its consequences might lead to the dissolution of the Union.

The Federalist orator drew special attention to the dangers from Indians that could result from turning down the British offer to transfer the posts in the Northwest to the Americans. Ames phrased his dramatic message as if it were being heard by the frontier settlers: ". . . in the daytime your path through the woods will be ambushed; the darkness of midnight will glitter with the blaze of your dwellings. You are a father — the blood of your son shall fatten your cornfield. You are a mother — the war whoop shall waken the sleep of the cradle. . . . By rejecting the posts we light the savage fires, we bind the victims."

At the end of this eloquent speech, Vice President John Adams, who was sitting in the gallery, said there was hardly a dry eye in the House. Some of the doubters who listened now were convinced that the future of the United States depended on the implementation of the Jay Treaty.

The day after Ames's address the treaty was sent to the Committee of the Whole. (This committee consists of the entire House membership meeting in a less-formal session.) Its chairman was Frederick Muhlenberg, a distinguished Pennsylvania congressman who had been Speaker of the House during the first session of Congress, 1789–1791, and again from 1793 through 1795. When the Committee of the Whole was asked to refer the treaty to the House for formal action, the vote was 49 to 49. Chairman Muhlenberg, although a Republican, then cast the tie-breaking vote in favor of the treaty. His bold action struck the House like a streak of lightning; Republican colleagues thundered their disbelief and disappointment.

A few days later Muhlenberg was attacked and stabbed with a knife by his own brother-in-law, a rabid Republican. The congressman recovered from his wounds, but his political career was ruined. His constituents branded him a "deserter," and Muhlenberg was driven from his House seat at the next election.

The opponents of the Jay Treaty still had not given up the fight. A resolution was introduced in the House to condemn the treaty as highly objectionable. The vote on it stood 48 to 48 until Speaker of the House Jonathan Dayton cast his vote against the measure. Then a less offensive resolution to label the treaty as simply objectionable was proposed. Once again the vote was a tie, and once again Speaker Dayton broke the tie with his negative vote.

Finally the organized opposition to the Jay Treaty petered out, and on April 30, 1796, the House voted 51 to 48 to provide the funds needed to implement it. The United States' first major foreign pact now went into operation, and the House failed to establish a precedent that it had the power to nullify treaties.

A Nonconformist in the Electoral College

For a few years in our history, during a period known as the Era of Good Feelings, the American people were politically united. By 1820 the Federalist party had passed into oblivion, and the United States had become a one-party nation. Republican James Monroe, who had swept to an easy victory in the 1816 presidential election, faced no opposition in his bid for reelection.

With only one candidate's name on the ballot, the 1820 election aroused little interest. Voting throughout the country was unusually light. In Richmond, Virginia, for example, only seventeen voters bothered to go to the polls.

It was a foregone conclusion that Monroe would win a unanimous victory in the electoral college. But political observers had not reckoned with the independence of one strong-willed elector, William Plumer of New Hampshire. Plumer had served his state as a senator and later as governor, so he was no political novice.

Plumer cast his electoral vote for noncandidate John Quincy Adams, Monroe's secretary of state. His lone vote robbed Monroe of duplicating the feat accomplished by George Washington, who gained every electoral vote in the presidential elections of 1789 and 1792.

Some people thought Plumer played the role of a spoiler because he felt that only Washington deserved the honor of being elected unanimously. But such was not the case. Plumer admired Adams and did not like Monroe. "My acquaintance with Mr. Adams has been long and intimate," he said. "I know he is in every respect qualified for that high trust. Mr. Monroe during the last four years has, in my opinion, conducted [himself] as president very improperly."

So William Plumer went his own way, content to be labeled a nonconformist in the electoral college.

God and Stephen Van Rensselaer

In 1824 there was still only the Republican party, but several prospective candidates for the presidency. In fact, shortly into Monroe's second term, politicians began jockeying for favorable positions. When Hezekiah Niles, the editor of *Niles' Weekly Register*, visited Washington in early 1822, he was surprised to find "so great a buz [sic] about the person who should succeed Mr. Monroe." A few months later Niles observed that the Washington lawmakers were giving much of their time to "electioneering for the next president of the United States."

If it had been within the power of Congress to select the next occupant of the White House, the choice would have been William H. Crawford of Georgia, the able secretary of the treasury. President Monroe favored Crawford as his successor and so did former Presidents Jefferson and Madison, but all three of them discreetly avoided taking an active role in the campaign.

Crawford's candidacy jumped off to a promising start, picking up strong support along most of the Atlantic Seaboard from Georgia through New York. But the early favorite's campaign was derailed by two stunning setbacks. First, Crawford was stricken with a paralytic stroke in September, 1823. Despite efforts to conceal his condition, it soon became evident that the secretary of the treasury was seriously ill. He was in bed for nearly eight weeks, unable even to sign official papers. When he finally returned to his office at the Treasury Department, Crawford was still very feeble. "He walks slowly like a blind man," wrote one observer.

Crawford's second setback occurred, ironically, when he was nominated for the presidency by the congressional caucus. Previous presidential candidates had been selected by party caucuses in Congress ever since the end of George Washington's administration. But by 1824 there was widespread opposition to the caucus method of choosing presidential nominees. Sarcastically labeled "King Caucus," it was assailed as undemocratic, dictatorial, and not representative of the will of the voters. So when the congressional caucus met in February 1824, only about a third of the members of Congress attended it; the other legislators boycotted this unpopular institution. As soon as Crawford became its candidate, unfriendly newspapers depicted him as the willing stooge of "King Caucus," and this lost him the support of many voters.

Several other candidates, nominated by state legislatures, entered the race against Crawford. One of the most formidable was Henry Clay, the eloquent, powerful Speaker of the House. A strong nationalist who wanted very much to be president (he ran again in 1832 and 1844), Clay was the only candidate with a clearly defined program of what he would do if elected. He called his plan the "American system" because it included some provisions for each section of the country. Clay proposed high protective tariffs that would benefit eastern manufacturers. The revenue from these tariffs would be spent on a transportation system needed by the West and on improving the navigation of southern rivers. Proudly nominated by the Kentucky legislature, Clay was hailed as the voice of the region then called the West.

But Clay had to contend with another authentic voice of the West, Andrew Jackson of Tennessee, who had served in both the House and the Senate. Jackson's fame, however, sprang more from his military exploits and dominant personality than from his political experience. Americans recalled how he had vanquished the Creek Indians in 1813, defeated the British at New Orleans in 1815, and pursued the Seminole Indians into Spanish Florida in 1818. "Old Hickory," moreover, was a classic example of the rags-to-riches hero who had pulled himself up by his own bootstraps from poverty and obscurity to wealth and fame. Although he was a prosperous plantation owner by the time he ran for the presidency, Jackson had become the symbol of the common man and the earnest champion of the new democratic spirit that was blossoming widely in the 1820s.

The candidate of the New England states was John Quincy Adams, the son of a president and, as secretary of state, the principal author of the Monroe Doctrine. For many years Adams had served his country with distinction on various foreign missions, in the Senate, and as head of the State Department. Brilliant and capable, Adams was regarded in the Northeast as a splendid, sensible presidential candidate. But the man from Massachusetts was also taciturn and aloof, and many voters in the western frontier states considered him too aristocratic. In the South Adams was generally unpopular because of his opposition to slavery and the likelihood that he would favor higher tariffs.

A fifth presidential candidate was Secretary of War John C. Calhoun of South Carolina. When it appeared that Calhoun had limited support outside his own state but was acceptable as a running mate to both the Adams and Jackson camps, he dropped out of the presidential race and instead concentrated his attention on seeking the vice presidency.

The four-cornered election was hard fought, and stalwart supporters of each candidate were involved in mudslinging. Crawford was attacked as too sick and inept to withstand the rigors of the presidency. Adams was castigated as stodgy, pompous, and an enemy of southern slave owners.

God and Stephen Van Rensselaer / 27

Clay was caricatured as a power-hungry drunkard and gambler. Jackson was called a murderer for having authorized the execution of two Scotsmen who were charged with inciting the Indians in the Seminole War. If all of these charges were to be believed, one astute politician observed that "our Presidents, Secretaries, Senators, and Representatives are all traitors and pirates, and the government of this people has been committed to the hands of public robbers."

Henry Clay said he was distraught because "the bitterness and violence of presidential electioneering increase as time advances. It seems as if every liar and calumniator in the country was at work day and night to destroy my character. . . ." But Clay himself was guilty of character assassination, repeatedly claiming that Andrew Jackson was a vile "military chieftain" totally unfit for the presidency.

The election began on October 29 and lasted until November 22. Each of the twenty-four states had its own election day, and because of this and the long distances between some of the states and Washington, D.C., the results were not known until the middle of December. Eighteen of the states selected their presidential electors by popular vote, the other six by legislatures. With four major candidates in the field, it appeared that none would win a majority of the electoral vote, and the election would then have to be decided by the House of Representatives.

New York, one of the states whose legislature still chose the electors, was considered the crucial, pivotal state. William Crawford was favored to win in New York, and if he could capture all or most of its 36 electoral votes (by far the largest bloc of votes of any state), he would be in a strong position if the election went to the House of Representatives. But the New York legislators disappointed Crawford by giving him only five electoral votes and 26 to their fellow Northerner, John Quincy Adams. Four New York votes went to Henry Clay and one to Andrew Jackson.

When the electoral votes of all the states were counted, New York was the only state that Adams carried except for the six New England states. Jackson was the winner in eleven states. In the electoral vote tally, Jackson led the field with 99, Adams was the runner-up with 84, Crawford had 41, and Clay 37. (Jackson also led in the popular vote with Adams again in second place.) Since no candidate received a majority of the electoral vote, by the terms of the Twelfth Amendment the House of Representatives had to choose the president from the three highest candidates.

Clay, finishing fourth in the race, was now out of the running. But because of his enormous influence in the House, he would become the kingmaker. While he delayed a public announcement of his choice, there was never any doubt in Clay's mind about whom he would support. Crawford was too incapacitated and not in favor of higher tariffs and internal improvements. Jackson was utterly loathed by Clay, who had even asked the House to condemn Old Hickory after his escapade in Spanish Florida. That left only Adams as the potential beneficiary of Clay's support. The personal habits of the two men were very different, but Clay respected Adams's intelligence and integrity, and they shared similar views on most foreign and domestic issues.

So Clay went to work for Adams, deftly gathering votes for him among his House colleagues. Each state had one vote in the House election, which meant it was necessary to win the support of a majority of congressmen within a state before it could be placed in any candidate's column.

When the balloting began on February 9, 1825, Adams won the six New England states, and, with Clay's help, he carried Kentucky, Ohio, Maryland, Illinois, Louisiana, and Missouri. That was twelve of the twenty-four states. But Adams needed one more state to win the presidency.

Attention again focused on New York as holding the key to the election. Half of the New York congressmen favored Adams; the other half were solidly for Crawford. The strategy of the managers of the Crawford campaign was to produce a tie in the New York delegation. This would prevent New York's ballot from being cast, deny Adams a first-ballot victory, and possibly lead to a deadlock that could only be broken by the eventual election of Crawford as a compromise candidate who was the second choice of many Adams and Jackson supporters.

One New York congressman whose vote the Crawford forces counted on was General Stephen Van Rensselaer, the aristocratic eighth patroon of the Dutch Manor of Rensselaer and the founder in 1824 of Rensselaer Polytechnic Institute. The elderly, pious Van Rensselaer had gone to the Capitol on election day prepared to vote for Crawford, but before he reached the House floor he was whisked into the Speaker's office by Clay and Daniel Webster. There he was told in no uncertain terms that the safety of the country depended on the election of Adams on the first ballot. Confronted by such eloquent persuaders as Clay and Webster, the old general emerged from the meeting confused and practically in tears.

In the corridor Van Rennselaer stopped Delaware Congressman Louis McLane and explained his predicament. "The election turns on me," he whispered in a nervous voice. "One vote will give Adams the majority—this is a responsibility I cannot bear. What shall I do?"

McLane counseled him to vote his conscience, and the general agreed that this was the honorable thing to do.

But when he took his seat in the House chamber, Van Rensselaer was still uncertain which way his conscience wanted him to vote. Deeply religious, he closed his eyes and bowed his head in prayer, seeking divine guidance. When he opened his eyes, he spotted a ballot that someone had dropped on the floor. It bore the name of John Quincy Adams. God had spoken to Stephen Van Rensselaer. Moments later he put the paper in the ballot box. New York thus cast 18 of its 34 votes for Adams, and the New Englander was elected president by winning 13 of the 24 states.

The election, however, was a real cliff-hanger for Adams. In five of the other states that he carried, a change of one vote would have deprived him of their support. John C. Calhoun, on the other hand, easily won election as vice president.

Jackson's partisans raged with fury. Their man had won the most electoral votes and the most popular votes but still was denied the presidency. (This never happened again in our history, although in the elections of 1876 and 1888 the candidate with the largest popular vote lost the presidency by finishing second in the electoral vote.)

Shortly after the election, Adams selected Clay as his secretary of state. This caused Jackson's supporters to accuse Adams and Clay of having made a "corrupt bargain" before the House decided the election. They charged that Adams had promised Clay the Cabinet position in return for Clay's help in winning the presidency. Jackson himself bitterly concluded that "the Judas of the West has closed the contract and will receive the thirty pieces of silver."

No evidence has ever been uncovered to substantiate the "corrupt bargain" charge. Apparently Adams was convinced that Clay, a man of many talents, would be a capable secretary of state. But the Jackson troops, growing in numbers with each passing year, did everything they could to make Adams's stay in the White House uncomfortable and unproductive. In 1828 they gained their revenge, winning Old Hickory the presidency in a landslide.

John Quincy Adams and his father, John Adams, were the only two of the first six presidents to be defeated for reelection. Like his father, the younger Adams was too distraught and disappointed to remain in Washington for the inauguration of his successor.

Calhoun Breaks a Tie and Reaps the "Tariff of Abominations"

As a strong nationalist in the early years of his political career, John C. Calhoun had ardently supported protective tariffs. In fact, when the 34-year-old congressman from South Carolina voted for the Tariff of 1816, he praised protective tariffs as "a most powerful cement" to hold the Union together. Young Calhoun firmly believed that his and other cotton-growing states soon would build their own textile plants and many other factories, too. When this happened, the South would become an industrialized region that could benefit from tariffs that raised the prices of competitive goods manufactured in Europe.

But as the years passed, few textile mills and factories were built in the South. By the mid-1820s it was obvious that South Carolina and the rest of the Old South—the seaboard area that had been settled first—had become the least prosperous section of the United States. The bustling Northeast was enjoying a boom in manufacturing, the developing West was flourishing from abundant wheat and corn crops, the frontier region of the Southwest was profiting from cotton freshly planted in rich new soil. But the cotton crop in the Old South, with its thin, overused soil, was petering out and not making much money for the plantation owners. John Randolph of Virginia testily remarked that masters would soon quit advertising for their runaway slaves, and slaves would begin advertising for their runaway masters.

Instead of blaming natural causes for much of their trouble, John Calhoun and other Southerners started attributing most of their woes to protective tariffs. They charged that the "Yankee tariffs" discriminated unfairly against them. Southerners sold their cotton at a low price to the North and Europe, but were forced to buy their manufactured goods at a price heavily inflated by tariffs. "We're selling our cotton dirt cheap," quipped one Southerner, "and buying our pots and pans sky high!"

In 1827, while Calhoun was serving as vice president in John Quincy Adams's administration, a higher tariff on woolens was proposed. When the Senate voted on this measure, there was a tie. Vice President Calhoun had his eye on the White House and knew that if he was ever to win the presidency, he would need to carry some of the manufacturing states. But his supporters back home in South Carolina never would forgive him for voting for a higher tariff. So when Calhoun was forced to cast the deciding ballot, he voted to kill the bill.

The defeat of this measure angered northern protectionists. In the next session of Congress, after an election in which many more Jacksonians won seats, the House Committee on Manufacturing began writing a new tariff bill. The Jacksonians then played an underhanded trick that they hoped would embarrass President Adams and the northern protectionists. They loaded the bill with so many ridiculously high duties (some as high as 45 percent of the value of the product) that they felt certain Congress would not pass it, and then they could blame the Adams supporters for its defeat.

But the New Englanders did not cave in as they were expected to do. Though they disliked many of the astronomically high duties—especially those on raw materials needed to manufacture products—a substantial number of Northerners bit the bullet and voted for the measure. To the surprise of many, the bill passed in both houses and became law on May 19, 1828.

When the startling news of the huge tariff increase reached Charleston, it was received with irate indignation. Flags were lowered to half mast; college students vowed to buy no northern goods; one Carolinian snickered, "Let the *New* England beware how she imitates the *Old*." Before long the Tariff of 1828 was known by a derisive nickname, the "Tariff of Abominations."

Calhoun fought back against what he considered to be a deliberate and reprehensible insult to his section of the country. He proposed a way to protect the minority in the South from what he called the "tyranny of the majority" in the North and West. Calhoun called for states to nullify within their own borders any laws that their citizens felt were unjust, oppressive, and unconstitutional. His theory of nullification was a dangerous doctrine aimed at crippling the effectiveness of the national government. And it foreshadowed catastrophic consequences that erupted many years later—the secession of the southern states and, finally, the war between the North and South.

Vice President Calhoun's tie-breaking vote against a moderate tariff measure in 1827 had triggered a whirlwind that could not be abated.

"Kill Him, Sir, Kill Him Dead"

Although Andrew Jackson ousted John Quincy Adams from the White House in the presidential election of 1828, Vice President John C. Calhoun was elected to a second term. At that time Calhoun and his new boss were good friends and political allies. Jackson toasted Calhoun in public as "an honest man, the noblest work of God," and asked his advice in choosing his Cabinet. Calhoun had every reason to believe that, with Jackson's blessing, he would become the next president of the United States.

Southerners, including Calhoun, were heartened by President Jackson's first annual message to Congress in December 1829. The president warned Congress against "all encroachments upon the legitimate sphere of state sovereignty." Advocates of states' rights considered this statement as evidence that Jackson would take their side in the growing controversy over nullification. But Old Hickory had something else in mind; he merely was opposed to the use of federal funds for roads and canals within the borders of any one state.

For several months President Jackson remained silent on the question of nullification. Finally, the states' righters decided to force him to take a stand on this controversial issue. They invited him to a banquet celebrating Thomas Jefferson's birth date on April 13, 1830. At the party twenty-four carefully prepared toasts were given, nearly all of them endorsing Calhoun's position favoring nullification. Then Jackson was called on to give a toast. The states' righters believed that the president, a southern plantation owner himself, would join those who had praised nullification.

Raising his glass, Jackson looked straight at Calhoun and emphatically declared, "Our Federal Union; it must be preserved." With these words the president made it clear that he had no patience with the idea that a state might nullify a national law. Vice President Calhoun was visibly shaken, and when his turn came to offer a toast, he muttered weakly, "The Union, next to our liberty, most dear."

From then on, the relations between the president and the vice president swiftly deteriorated. Shortly after the Jefferson Day party, Jackson discovered that in the past Calhoun had betrayed him on a sensitive matter. Previously, Jackson had presumed that Calhoun had supported his conduct of the Seminole War in 1818. But now the president learned the truth from a letter written by William Crawford. Calhoun, who had been secretary of war in 1818, had argued in secret Cabinet sessions for Jackson's court martial following the Tennessee general's unauthorized invasion of Spanish Florida.

Jackson now demanded a full explanation from his vice president. So Calhoun wrote a lengthy defense of his actions and then, hoping to gain public sympathy, released this information to the press. Jackson was furious that Calhoun had turned this private matter into a public exposé, and he found the vice president's explanation totally unsatisfactory. "Understanding you now," Jackson wrote curtly, "no further communication with you on this subject is necessary." This episode made it impossible for the president ever again to trust the honesty and loyalty of the vice president.

The breach between the two top men in the government was made complete by an ugly personal affair. The barmaid daughter of a Washington innkeeper, pretty Peggy O'Neale, had married Major John H. Eaton, one of Jackson's cronies. When Eaton was appointed secretary of war by Jackson, his ambitious wife was determined to become a full-fledged lady of society. But Mrs. Calhoun and the wives of the Cabinet members repeatedly snubbed her. They called Peggy Eaton an ill-bred hussy and hinted that she had bestowed sexual favors on many men during her barmaid days. The blue-blooded Mrs. Calhoun refused to attend any of the Eatons' parties and led the feminine plot to exclude Mrs. Eaton from all the official social functions.

President Jackson, however, came to the defense of Peggy Eaton. Partly because of his wife's own unfortunate experience, the president was extremely sensitive about women who were subjected to slander. Rachel Jackson had been accused of adultery and bigamy. This was because when she married Andrew Jackson, she mistakenly thought her first husband had already divorced her, but he had never bothered to file the case in court. Later the divorce was obtained and the Jacksons repeated their marriage vows. But for the rest of her life Rachel Jackson was dogged by cruel scandalmongers, and the president felt that this ceaseless barrage of criticism contributed to her failing health and finally to her death a few months before his inauguration. So President Jackson had good reason to champion the cause of Peggy Eaton and scorn her enemies.

Washington gossips reveled in every juicy morsel of the Eaton affair, which newspapers dubbed the "Petticoat War." The president's own niece, Mrs. Andrew Donelson, resigned as White House hostess rather than call on the innkeeper's daughter. Even the diplomatic corps became involved in the conflict. The wife of the minister from Holland would not sit at the same table with Mrs. Eaton. However, the British and Russian ministers, both bachelors, were delighted to attend the Eatons' parties. (These parties often were lively affairs; at one of them Mrs. Eaton engaged in a brief fistfight with a matron she thought had insulted her.)

While the wives of most of the Cabinet members enlisted their husbands in the anti-Eaton campaign, they were unable to lasso the widower who was secretary of state, Martin Van Buren. A balding, sharp-featured little man, Van Buren was one of the shrewdest, most skillful politicians in our nation's history. In New York state he developed and commanded the country's first large effective political machine. And his own credentials as an officeholder were very impressive. Van Buren had served as a state senator, state attorney general, United States senator, and governor of New York before resigning his gubernatorial post to accept appointment in Jackson's Cabinet.

The Eaton affair played directly into the hands of Van Buren. The secretary of state readily accepted Mrs. Eaton's party invitations and showered her with kindly attention. This greatly pleased the old general in the White House, who already had formed a close attachment to the New Yorker and fondly called him "Matty." While Jackson's opinion of Calhoun continued declining, his favorable impression of Van Buren grew more pronounced. Soon he was grooming the New Yorker as his probable running mate in the 1832 elections, and, looking beyond his own presidency, Jackson considered Matty the man best qualified to succeed him in the White House. "Van Buren was not an intriguer," Jackson said, "but frank, open, candid, and manly; an able and prudent councilor, pleasant, and well qualified to fill the highest office in the gift of the people.... I wish I could say as much for Mr. Calhoun."

Before long the newspapers were filled with rumors that Van Buren was Jackson's heir apparent. While Matty looked forward to the day when he could hold a higher office, he felt that these constant rumors would make him appear too eager and presumptuous. So, claiming that "premature agitation" leaves the administration "embarrassed and weakened," Van Buren resigned as secretary of state. A short time later Eaton left the Cabinet, too. This gave President Jackson a good excuse for ridding the Cabinet of all the disloyal opponents of Peggy Eaton, and he procured the resignation of every member except the postmaster general.

A reorganized Cabinet was formed with an eye to harmony. Among the new appointees were Attorney General Roger B. Taney, who later became the Supreme Court chief justice that handed down the famous Dred Scott decision, and Secretary of War Lewis Cass, who became the Democratic nominee for president in 1848.

Calhoun and Van Buren's other political enemies, including Henry Clay and Daniel Webster, were delighted that the New Yorker was no longer in the Cabinet. They felt that he would soon fade from the limelight and lose the clout that he had wielded in Jackson's administration.

But speculation about the demise of Van Buren's political career was premature. The day after he left the State Department, Matty was appointed minister to Great Britain. It was an interim appointment and would not become official until the Senate had given its advice and consent, which could not occur at that time because the Senate was not in session. The next session of Congress would not begin until five months later.

A fascinating question was circulating in Capitol corridors. Had the wily Van Buren outfoxed his opponents by helping President Jackson get rid of his unwanted Cabinet members and, in the process, solidified his high standing with Old Hickory? (No wonder Van Buren's enemies called him the "Little Magician"!) With the opportunity for continued public exposure as minister to the Court of St. James, Van Buren might still be tapped as Jackson's running mate in 1832 and as a presidential nominee in 1836.

Calhoun, Clay, and Webster all coveted the presidency, so these three master politicians decided to gang up on Van Buren. When his appointment as minister to Great Britain came up for Senate confirmation, they would try to get it rejected. Clay and Webster were both powerful senators who could exert much influence on their colleagues from the West and North, while Vice President Calhoun held the southern senators in the grasp of his hand. Their plot had a good chance to succeed. If it did, the conspirators felt that it would completely humiliate the Little Magician and end his quest for a higher office.

When Van Buren's name came before the Senate for confirmation, the senators debated for two days in secret session. Clay accused Van Buren of making unfavorable concessions to the British while negotiating trade treaties. He also attacked the New Yorker for promoting the spoils system and ruling as a dictator in his home state. Other senators referred disparagingly to the compromising role that Van Buren had played in the Eaton affair. But the charge that was the most damaging was that President Jackson should not have given Van Buren an interim appointment and then asked the Senate to approve it five months later. The president, many senators believed, had stretched his power too far, and the Senate must not submit to the will of "King Andrew."

The tide against Van Buren's nomination mounted steadily. When the conspirators felt certain they had enough votes to defeat the nomination, they staged the balloting as if it were a climax to an exciting drama.

They permitted only enough senators on the floor to assure that the vote would be tied. This was contrived to give Vice President Calhoun the honor and pleasure of casting the deciding vote that would bring Van Buren home from London in humiliation.

When the tie vote was announced, the vice president stepped down from the dais with solemn dignity. Senator Thomas Hart Benton of Missouri later said that Calhoun seemed to relish this crucial moment as the opportunity to destroy his political foe. Benton claimed that just before Calhoun cast his negative vote, the vice president said to a friend, "It will kill him, sir, kill him dead. He will never kick, sir, never kick."

Benton, a Jackson-Van Buren supporter, had a much different opinion about the future effect of Calhoun's decisive vote. Turning to Senator Gabriel Moore of Alabama, Benton declared, "You have broken a minister and elected a vice president."

"Good God!" replied Moore. "Why didn't you tell me that before I voted?"

Benton's prophecy proved to be correct. Many people felt that the Senate's rejection of Van Buren was a cheap and despicable political trick. The popularity of the Little Magician suddenly soared upward. In Tennessee, for example, before the Senate voted, Van Buren was not widely known. But a frontier politician said that after the Senate acted, many Tennesseans became aware of Jackson's New York friend. "Two men know him now," he surmised, "to one that knew him sixty days ago."

Nominated for the vice presidency in 1832, Van Buren was easily elected, and four years later he won the presidency. In March 1837, Jackson happily handed Matty the keys to the White House. (This proved to be an unusual event. In the next 150 years no incumbent president, except in the case of his death or resignation, was succeeded by his own vice president.)

Calhoun, Clay, and Webster all failed to become president. Calhoun did not even complete his term as Jackson's vice president. In December 1832, he was chosen by the South Carolina legislature to fill a vacancy in the Senate. Calhoun then resigned as vice president but stayed on in Washington to battle in Congress for states' rights and nullification.

Nearly a century and a half passed before another vice president resigned his office. This was Spiro T. Agnew, who stepped down in 1973 after he was charged with illegal financial transactions.

The Only Vice President Elected by the Senate

Some significant political changes occurred in the 1830s. During this decade the party that had been founded by Jefferson and Madison changed its name from Republican to Democratic. The first president to call himself a Democrat was Andrew Jackson, who had a charismatic appeal to the "common man" and a large army of devoted followers. But his overbearing manner and controversial policies drew only contempt and hatred from other Americans. During the 1830s many anti-Jackson factions came together to help form a new political party, the Whigs. Also, in this same decade political conventions replaced state legislatures (and the earlier congressional caucuses) as the vehicle for nominating presidential and vice presidential candidates.

Jackson ruled over the Democratic party with an iron fist. To put an end to speculation about his successor in the White House, he ordered his party to hold its nominating convention in May 1835, eighteen months before the next presidential election. The president had no problem getting the convention to accept his protégé, Vice President Martin Van Buren, to head the ticket. Van Buren won the votes of all 265 delegates. But Jackson's hand-picked candidate for the vice presidency, Colonel Richard M. Johnson of Kentucky, was not received enthusiastically by the convention.

Johnson was a colorful and experienced politician who had first been elected to the House of Representatives in 1807. When the War of 1812 began, Johnson left his seat in Congress, joined the Kentucky volunteers as a colonel, and fought in the West under the command of General William Henry Harrison. While charging the Indian allies of the British, Johnson was severely wounded, but the American forces prevailed and he was borne from the field a hero. During the fighting he had killed an Indian chief reputed to be the famous Tecumseh.

After his wounds healed, Johnson returned to Congress and assumed new prominence as the alleged slayer of Tecumseh. In 1816 he secured the passage of a measure he proposed that gave congressmen an annual salary of $1,500 instead of the small daily allowance they had been receiving. This, he believed, would encourage congressmen to be more responsible and efficient, but voters looked upon it instead as a selfish "salary grab" and turned out of office many members who had supported it. Johnson held on to his own seat only by bowing to the will of the people and working for the repeal of his own bill.

Johnson was a member of the House until 1819, a senator from 1819 to 1829, and a congressman again from 1829 to 1837. All of this time he was a loyal supporter and confidant of President Jackson. When the question of Jackson's conduct in the Seminole War of 1818 was before the House, Johnson was the only member of the Committee on Military Affairs to speak in favor of Old Hickory. While Jackson was in the White House, Johnson consistently voted for the bills that the president wanted passed. And the Kentucky colonel even acted as Jackson's personal agent in pressuring the Cabinet members to encourage their wives to accept Peggy Eaton in their social circle. So it was quite logical for Jackson to urge the 1836 Democratic convention to nominate his close friend for the vice presidency.

But Colonel Johnson had a serious flaw in the eyes of many convention delegates. When his father had died, Johnson received as part of his inheritance a young black slave named Julia Chinn. Johnson decided to take Chinn as his mistress, and by her he had two children. When he went to Washington, Johnson was accompanied by Chinn and he referred to her as his wife. The society matrons refused to accept her at their parties, so Johnson seldom went to social affairs.

Julia Chinn died during a cholera epidemic in Kentucky in 1833. Then Johnson, who never married, took other black slaves as mistresses.

Johnson's total disregard of the social conventions prevalent at that time greatly offended large numbers of convention delegates, especially those from the South. When his name was placed in nomination for the vice presidential spot, it was greeted with loud hisses from the Virginia delegation. And when it came time for the delegates to vote on his candidacy, Johnson received 178 votes, just one vote more than the required two-thirds majority.

Nevertheless, the colonel's supporters waged a vigorous campaign in his behalf. They played to the hilt the notion that he had killed Tecumseh. For this alleged feat in his past, Johnson was nicknamed "the Hero of the Thames," and a campaign biography boasted about his valor on the battlefield. A play was written that celebrated his murder of the Indian chief, and Johnson saw it and applauded wildly. Democrats even sang this silly ditty:

> Rumpsey dumpsey, rumpsey dumpsey,
> Colonel Johnson killed Tecumseh.

In 1836 the Whigs had not yet become a unified party. They felt they didn't have candidates with enough nationwide appeal to run successfully against the Van Buren–Johnson ticket. So the Whigs decided to support favorite sons in various parts of the country with the hope that their combined electoral vote could deny the Democrats victory and force the election into the House of Representatives, where they would then unite behind the most popular candidate.

Thus, Democrat Van Buren ran against three Whig presidential candidates: Massachusetts Senator Daniel Webster in the North, Senator Hugh L. White of Tennessee in the South, and General William Henry Harrison in the West. Democrat Johnson also had three opponents for the vice presidency: Whig Francis Granger of New York, Whig John Tyler of Virginia, and an independent southern Democrat, William Smith of Alabama.

Van Buren won the presidency with 170 electoral votes against a combined total of 124 electoral votes for the three Whig candidates. His running mate, Johnson, was not so fortunate. Virginia's 23 electors cast their ballots for Van Buren for the top office, but they deserted the Democratic nominee for the vice presidency. So Johnson won only 147 electoral votes; his three opponents combined also had 147 electoral votes. The Kentucky colonel thus was one electoral vote short of being elected vice president.

Because Johnson did not win a majority of the electoral vote, the Senate, for the first and only time in American history, had to elect the vice president. (When the House of Representatives has to choose the president, each state has a single vote; when the Senate has to select the vice president, each senator has one vote.) The suspense finally ended when the Senate elected Johnson by a margin of 33 votes to 16 for Granger, who had finished second in the electoral-vote count.

While Johnson served as vice president, he continued to have black concubines. When one of them proved unfaithful, he put her up for sale and then took her sister as his next mistress.

In 1840 the Democrats ran President Van Buren for reelection, but they considered Johnson morally unfit and refused to nominate him for a second term. Instead, the party chieftains told the state Democratic leaders that there would be no national candidate for the vice presidency; the states were free to nominate their own vice presidential candidates.

Not that it made much difference. Van Buren lost the 1840 presidential election to Whig candidate William Henry Harrison, whose vice presidential running mate was John Tyler. When the young Whig party captured the White House, the era of Jacksonian rule had finally come to an end.

A Vice President Helps Polk Keep His Pledge

William Henry Harrison had the shortest tenure in office of any president. He caught cold during the inauguration day ceremonies, developed pneumonia, and died one month later. John Tyler then became the first vice president to be elevated to the country's highest office by the death of the elected president.

Tyler was a Virginia Whig, and he had been placed on the ticket as Harrison's running mate chiefly to attract southern votes. A believer in states' rights, President Tyler clashed repeatedly with the western and northern Whigs led by Senator Henry Clay and Secretary of State Daniel Webster. This intraparty warfare came to a head when Tyler twice vetoed a bill to reestablish the Bank of the United States, a project strongly supported by Clay and most Cabinet members. When Tyler refused to accept the bank measure, the Whigs in his Cabinet were furious and all except Webster resigned. Clay even resigned in disgust from the Senate.

The split between President Tyler and the Whig leaders badly damaged the party, and the Democrats gained many seats in the congressional elections of 1842. When the presidential election of 1844 approached, the Whigs refused to run Tyler for a second term (he was the first incumbent president not to be nominated for reelection). The party turned instead to Clay as its 1844 standard-bearer.

Former President Martin Van Buren was heavily favored to win the Democratic presidential nomination. But shortly before the convention, Van Buren announced that he opposed the annexation of Texas, which had won its freedom from Mexico in 1836. Southerners were eager to have Texas annexed, since it would add to the Union a vast cotton-growing region. But antislavery Northerners were just as determined to keep Texas out of the Union. So when Van Buren sided with the North on this inflammatory issue, he lost nearly all of his southern support at the Democratic convention.

Even so, Van Buren managed to win a simple majority of the votes on the first convention ballot, but he was far short of the two-thirds margin needed to win the nomination. On succeeding roll calls Van Buren's strength declined, but his chief opponent, Lewis Cass of Michigan, also was unable to muster two-thirds of the votes.

When the convention deadlocked, delegates turned to a compromise candidate. On the ninth ballot they nominated former Governor James K. Polk of Tennessee. Polk became the first dark horse candidate in

American history to win a presidential nomination. He favored the annexation of Texas, which assured him of southern support, but he was so little known throughout the country that the Whigs gleefully asked, "Who is James K. Polk?"

Senator Silas Wright of New York was selected by a nearly unanimous vote as the Democratic vice presidential nominee. However, Wright was a friend of Van Buren, and he was angry because the convention had bypassed Matty. So he refused the nomination, speedily notifying the delegates by way of Samuel Morse's new invention, the telegraph.

Then the convention selected George M. Dallas of Pennsylvania as its replacement for Wright. Dallas had been mayor of Philadelphia, a senator, and later the American minister to Russia.

The election was hard fought and extremely close. New York was the crucial state. The Polk-Dallas ticket eked out a narrow victory in New York, carrying the state by about 5,000 votes out of more than 485,000 votes cast. The Democrats' New York win was due in large part to a third-party candidate, James G. Birney, who siphoned off many potential votes for Clay. Running for the antislavery Liberty party, Birney received 15,812 votes, most of which probably would have gone to Clay if Birney had not been in the race. If the Democrats had lost New York, Clay would have won enough electoral votes to achieve his never-fulfilled dream of becoming president.

Bitter because his own Whig party had abandoned him, outgoing President Tyler supported Democrat Polk in the 1844 election. When Polk was declared the winner, Tyler interpreted his victory as a clear signal that the voters wanted Texas annexed, and shortly before he left office, Tyler pushed through Congress a joint resolution adding Texas to the Union.

The day that Polk moved into the White House he told one of his Cabinet members that he had four goals he wanted to accomplish as president:

> (1) annex California, which was then owned by Mexico; (2) settle with Great Britain the question of who would control the huge Oregon territory; (3) reestablish the Independent Treasury System, whereby the federal government would collect its taxes in gold and silver and store this specie in vaults throughout the country (this had been started by the Democrats in 1840 but abolished by the Whigs in 1842); (4) lower the tariff, which had been substantially raised by the Whigs in 1842.

In accord with Polk's goals, the United States annexed California as part of the peace terms that ended the Mexican War in 1848. The Oregon

42 / By a Single Vote!

question was peaceably resolved in 1846 when Great Britain and the United States agreed to divide the territory along the forty-ninth parallel. As a result of President Polk's prodding, Congress voted to restore the Independent Treasury System in 1846.

Reducing the tariff, however, was a hard nut for Polk to crack. When Treasury Secretary Robert J. Walker recommended a measure to revise rates downward, most Whigs in Congress opposed it, and so did some prominent Democrats from the northern industrial states. The bill passed in the Democratic-controlled House, but it ran into trouble in the Senate, where the membership was more closely divided between the two major parties.

Four northern Democratic senators joined the Whigs in voting against the Walker Tariff, and when the vote total was announced, the result was a 27-27 tie. The success or failure of the measure then rested squarely on the shoulders of Vice President George M. Dallas.

The vice president faced a tough decision. Personally Dallas was a protectionist, like many other officeholders from Pennsylvania. But his president and party had pledged to reduce the tariff. When he finally cast the tie-breaking ballot, Dallas voted for the Walker Tariff. Some of his friends objected strenuously, but the vice president defended his decisive action on the ground that as a national officer he must obey the platform of his party.

Dallas's crucial vote enabled President Polk to achieve in one term all four goals he had set at the beginning of his administration. Having fulfilled his ambition, Polk had no desire to run for reelection, and he gladly relinquished the presidency after four years in office.

When historians are surveyed about the relative effectiveness of American presidents, they often put James K. Polk in the "near-great" category. Polk was not as brilliant, beloved, or dynamic as some other men who have occupied the White House, but he was a hard-working, determined chief executive who did all he said he would do. How many other presidents have matched that record?

A Whiff of Glory

In 1854 the modern Republican party was born, and soon it replaced the rapidly fading Whigs as one of America's two major political parties. When the Thirty-sixth Congress convened in 1859, the Republicans had gained control of the House of Representatives and made deep inroads into the Democrats' lead in the Senate.

But when the House members tried to select their Speaker, a long heated struggle occurred. The bitter fight lasted for two months and took forty-four ballots to resolve. While the battle continued, congressmen shouted nasty oaths at each other, and some of them actually brandished pistols and knives.

Eventually all the leading contenders fell by the wayside, and urgent pleas were made to find a compromise choice. Someone suggested that William Pennington of New Jersey might be considered. But the problem with Pennington was that he was a new member of the House and virtually unknown to most of his colleagues.

Pennington showed no special aptitude for leadership, but, on the other hand, he had not been in Congress long enough to make many enemies. So when the representatives voted on him, Pennington was elected Speaker by a one-vote margin, with 117 congressmen voting yes and 116 congressmen voting no.

The only other first-term congressman elected Speaker of the House was Henry Clay. But there the similarity between Clay and Pennington ends. While Clay etched a long and enviable record in both the House and Senate, William Pennington served only one brief term as Speaker.

In fact, poor Pennington's descent to obscurity was just as fast as his climb to fame—he wasn't even reelected to a second term in the House.

A President Stands Trial

No vice president was ever elevated to the presidency under more adverse conditions than those that confronted Andrew Johnson when he took the oath of office on April 15, 1865. The previous night Abraham Lincoln had been assassinated. How could any successor adequately fill the shoes of the martyred president? Moreover, less than a week had passed since Robert E. Lee surrendered his rebel army to Ulysses S. Grant at Appomattox, and Union forces were still fighting the Confederates in North Carolina, Alabama, and Louisiana. But the final curtain was at last coming down on America's most devastating and tragic war. A once strong, united nation had been severed into two warring sides, each loathing the other. Confusion ruled in the victorious North; chaos and helplessness reigned in the prostrate South. Ahead lay the immensely difficult task of restoring and reconstructing the battered Union.

Abraham Lincoln had been expected to undertake this formidable task. But the assassin's bullet that felled Lincoln suddenly shifted the burden onto the shoulders of a man who seemed ill equipped for its demands. The new president lacked Lincoln's broad-minded judgment, unerring tact, and remarkable capacity to compromise differences. And besides his personal weaknesses, Johnson already had two strikes against him when he assumed the presidency. He himself had been a slave-owning Southerner, yet he now headed the government dedicated to bringing about the eradication of slavery and the submission of the South. And to make matters worse, Johnson was a Democrat serving in a Republican administration that scorned his party as a collection of Copperhead scoundrels in the North and Confederate traitors in the South.

In at least one way, however, Johnson was like Lincoln. Both presidents reached the White House from humble beginnings. Born to poor parents in North Carolina in 1808 (the year before Lincoln's birth), Johnson was orphaned early and never had the chance to attend school. Instead, he was apprenticed at age ten to a tailor. The understanding was that he would remain an indentured servant until his twenty-first birthday. He learned the tailoring trade and taught himself to read. But the boy was made miserable by his overbearing employer, so he ran away and tramped for many miles through the Carolina woods. Although his employer offered a reward for his return, young Johnson could not be found.

In 1826 he moved to the mountainous region of east Tennessee and settled in the town of Greeneville. Here he started his own tailor shop and married Eliza McCardle, the daughter of a Scottish shoemaker. She helped her husband improve his reading and taught Johnson to write and do simple arithmetic.

In time his tailor shop became modestly successful, but Johnson never acquired the wealth and social position that came to some of the big plantation owners with their large armies of slaves. Although Johnson had a few slaves himself, he strongly resented the rich planter aristocracy. In the late 1820s the town tailor became interested in politics and campaigned as a Jacksonian Democrat. Johnson first became a town alderman, then mayor of Greeneville, and later a member of the state legislature.

In 1843 the medium-built, dark-eyed, black-haired Tennessean began his first of five consecutive terms in the House of Representatives. His most notable achievement as a congressman was the introduction of the first homestead bill to divide western lands into small, free tracts for farmers. But this bill was defeated by southern representatives who defended the interests of the large landholders.

Johnson was elected governor of Tennessee in 1853 and reelected in 1855. In this position he convinced the legislature to provide the first tax in Tennessee for public education, and he established a state board of education and a state library. By the mid-1850s Johnson was well known as a champion of the underdog. Throughout his career he supported the small white farmers in their ceaseless battle against the large landowners. He always fought against any claims of superiority based on birth or wealth.

In 1857, at the time when the schism between the North and South was widening dangerously, Johnson won election to the Senate. When the eleven southern states seceded in 1860 and 1861, the Tennessean attracted the attention of the North by his outspoken arguments for the preservation of the Union. But Johnson's pleas went unheeded, and he was the only southern senator who did not resign and go back to his state when it seceded.

After the Union forces won some battles in Tennessee and liberated part of that state from southern control, President Lincoln appointed Johnson military governor of Tennessee in March 1862. The following year the last Confederate troops were driven from Tennessee, and Johnson set out to restore a civil government in the first state to drop out of the Confederacy.

Despite the important Union victories at Gettysburg and Vicksburg in 1863, as the presidential election of 1864 approached, the Republican party was in deep trouble. The war was still dragging on, and there was little prospect that the Union armies would soon destroy the Confederacy. Some Northerners accused Lincoln of not pursuing the war with the determination and superior strategy needed to bring it to a successful conclusion; other Northerners adamantly attacked the president for not ending the bloodshed and proposing a negotiated settlement that would let the Southerners go their own way.

The feelings against his administration were so intense that Lincoln felt quite certain he would not be elected for a second term. Republican leaders, thinking their situation was desperate, decided that the best chance of reelecting Lincoln was to bid for a large vote from the northern Democrats who still supported the Union war effort. They called their new allies "War Democrats" and nominated for the vice presidency a Democrat who had demonstrated his persisting loyalty to the United States — Andrew Johnson. The Republicans were so eager to publicize the fusion between their party and the loyal Democrats that they shed their party name for the 1864 elections and announced that the Lincoln-Johnson ticket ran under the banner of the Union party.

Shortly before the election, the northern armies won some very important victories in the field. General William T. Sherman took Atlanta, and General Philip K. Sheridan defeated large Confederate forces in the Shenandoah Valley. Amidst soaring hopes that the end of the war was now in sight, the Lincoln-Johnson campaign suddenly caught fire. The Democrats, on the other hand, had a vexing problem because their presidential nominee, General George B. McClellan, refused to endorse the peace plank in his party platform. On election day the Union party reelected its Republican president and elected its Democratic vice president.

In his Second Inaugural Address, Lincoln expressed his fervent wish that the war would be followed by a charitable, merciful peace. "With malice toward none," he declared, "with charity for all, with firmness in the right as God gives us to see the right, let us strive on to finish the work we are in, to bind up the nation's wounds, to care for him who shall have borne the battle and for his widow and orphan, to do all which may achieve and cherish a just and lasting peace among ourselves and with all nations."

Long before his second term in the White House began, Lincoln had been thinking about the question of how to readmit southern states to the Union after the war was over. In 1863 he proposed a solution to this question. Each state's readmittance would be considered individually. As a first step, a group of voters equal to 10 percent of the voting population of the southern state in 1860 must sign an oath of allegiance to the United States. The next step would be the creation of a new state government under a constitution that eliminated slavery. Then the United States would permit this state to rejoin the Union. Lincoln made no specific demands for the treatment of the black people in the readmitted southern states other than to insist that their freedom must be observed.

Actually, the Great Emancipator did not foresee how most of the black people, lacking employable skills or property, could fit into the mainstream of American life. He suggested the totally impractical idea that they might be transported as colonists to Africa and the Caribbean countries. Vice President Johnson's ideas about the blacks were even more naive and nearsighted than Lincoln's. While he favored their emancipation, Johnson considered the blacks inferior people. When he became president, Johnson did not advocate giving the vote and full civil rights to all black males, nor did he support most of the programs intended to provide economic help and education for the freed slaves. This stubborn adherence to a caste system was one of the significant reasons why the Johnson administration was plagued with turbulence and turmoil.

Some northern congressmen and senators, who came to be called Radical Republicans, felt that President Lincoln's policy toward the South was too lenient and his attitude toward the blacks too indifferent. It was absurd, they said, to consider an ex-Confederate state loyal to the United States when only 10 percent of its male voters pledged their allegiance to the national government. Even during the Civil War at least 10 percent of the people in any southern state opposed secession and sympathized with the northern cause! And what was to happen to the freed blacks if the United States government made no provisions to protect them from the vengeful acts of their former masters? Moreover, the Radical Republicans claimed that Congress, not the president, should determine reconstruction policies. During the Civil War President Lincoln had assumed more power than any previous American president; now that the emergency had passed, Congress wanted to reassert its powers as a co-equal branch of the government.

The Radical Republicans in 1864 had maneuvered through Congress the Wade-Davis Bill, which called for much harsher conditions for readmitting the southern states to the Union. When Lincoln killed the bill by a pocket veto, the Radicals accused the president of a "studied outrage on the legislative authority of the people." They demanded that Lincoln "confine himself to his executive duties . . . and leave political organization to Congress."

So the battle lines over reconstruction were clearly drawn between the president and the Radical Republicans before Lincoln was assassinated. When Johnson first assumed the presidency, some of the Radicals believed that the new chief executive shared their views about how the defeated South should be treated. Less than a week after he took office, President Johnson expressed his belief "that treason must be made odious, that traitors must be punished and impoverished. They must not only be punished, but their social power must be destroyed."

The Radicals relished these scathing remarks by the new president, but they sadly misjudged his overall position on reconstruction. When

Johnson had demanded that traitors be punished, he had in mind the elite group of rich plantation owners he had always despised. Under Lincoln's reconstruction plan virtually all of the rebels were to be pardoned immediately except those who had held high civil or military posts in the Confederacy and those who had resigned from similar posts in the United States government to help the southern cause. To this group barred from immediate pardons Johnson, venting his hatred for the slave-owning aristocracy, added all Southerners with taxable property worth more than $20,000. However, the new president reserved the right to pardon any Confederates whose personal pleas he found acceptable.

Overall, the Johnson and Lincoln plans were very similar, and in the summer of 1865 Johnson encouraged the Southerners to follow his instructions for forming new state governments. First, Johnson said, special state conventions were to be called. These conventions had to repeal the ordinances of secession, repudiate debts incurred in the war, and ratify the slave-freeing Thirteenth Amendment. Then the states would be readmitted to the Union and could elect senators and representatives to Congress.

In the second half of 1865, new southern state governments were rapidly organized under the generous terms of the Johnson plan. Congress was not in session at this time, but the Radicals watched with horror the events unfolding in the South. State after state enacted laws known as Black Codes that were designed to let the southern whites control the emancipated slaves. Blacks were forced to make long-term contracts with white employers; if they tried to break these contracts, they could be ordered to forfeit their back wages or be dragged to work by paid "Negro catchers." Those blacks without steady jobs could be arrested for vagrancy, and either their labor was sold to the highest bidder or they were sentenced to work in chain gangs. Blacks were not allowed to vote or serve on juries, no schools were open to them, and in some states they were not permitted to rent or lease land. The Black Codes upheld the principle of white supremacy, which was aptly described by the governor of Mississippi, who said, "Ours is and ever shall be a government of white men."

In addition to the anger generated by the Black Codes, the Radical Republicans were infuriated when they learned that President Johnson had pardoned large numbers of Confederate leaders and the southern states had willfully and insolently elected many of them to Congress. Among the southern delegations waiting to take their seats in the House and Senate were four southern generals and five colonels, plus several Cabinet members from the Confederate government, and even Alexander

Stephens, vice president of the Confederacy, who had been indicted for treason.

When the Republican-dominated Congress convened in December 1865, it refused to seat the senators and representatives elected from the South. Then the congressional leaders formed a Joint Committee on Reconstruction, composed of members of both houses. This committee was charged with the responsibility of drawing up bills that would determine the course of reconstruction. Thus, the Radical Republicans shot off their opening salvo in a bitter, prolonged war with the president over who would control the future of the South.

The Radicals undoubtedly were motivated both by idealism and self-interest. Some, like Senator Charles Sumner of Massachusetts, felt a genuine concern for the black people who had emerged from bondage but who, with few skills and no educational opportunities, were now free to starve in the economically devastated South. Sumner believed that the national government must provide the blacks with economic help, education, and political rights. They needed the ballot both for their own protection against the whites and to enable them to assume civic responsibilities. But there were other Radicals whose chief interest in giving the vote to blacks and withholding it from thousands of ex-Confederates was to keep their own party in power. As long as the grateful freedmen voted Republican and large numbers of southern Democrats were disfranchised, the Republican party could control both ends of Pennsylvania Avenue.

Sumner spearheaded the Radicals' program in the Senate, and his counterpart in the House of Representatives was Thaddeus Stevens of Pennsylvania, who harbored a deep hatred for the South and regarded the former Confederate states as "conquered provinces." The first bill that the Radicals pushed through Congress enlarged the powers of the Freedmen's Bureau, a federal relief agency that provided aid primarily for the former slaves. President Johnson vetoed the bill, stating that it was an unconstitutional invasion of the rights of the southern states. The Radicals failed to override this veto by the slim margin of two votes in the Senate (later the bill was passed again and the president's veto was overridden). Then the Radicals passed a sweeping Civil Rights Act, promising blacks the protection of their rights in federal courts. Johnson vetoed it because he said it violated states' rights, but Congress overrode his veto.

The next item on the Radicals' agenda was extremely important: the Fourteenth Amendment. Its first section says that a state may not "deprive any person of life, liberty, or property without due process of law, nor deny to any person within its jurisdiction the equal protection of the laws." Originally this section was intended to guarantee the citizenship and civil rights of the blacks in case the Civil Rights Act of 1866 later was declared unconstitutional. Another section of the Fourteenth Amendment would deprive the southern states of their full representation in Congress and the electoral college if they denied black males the vote. This amendment also excluded from public office all ex-Confederates who had previously held any government position that required them to take an oath to support the U.S. Constitution, unless they were pardoned by a two-thirds vote of both houses of Congress.

A president cannot veto a constitutional amendment, but Johnson strongly disapproved of the section that forbade the southern people to elect to office those men they looked upon as their true leaders. So he urged the southern states not to ratify the Fourteenth Amendment.

This was a serious blunder. It incurred the wrath of the Radicals without helping the position of the Southerners. The president would have done less harm to his own career and to the South had he advised the southern states to accept the Fourteenth Amendment as the best they could get from a Congress controlled by Northerners.

Johnson and the Radicals came out of their corners swinging during the congressional elections campaign of 1866. The president made a tour covering much of the country—called a "swing around the circle"—in which he journeyed 2,000 miles and delivered eleven major and twenty-two minor speeches. Johnson appealed to the crowds to support his merciful policies toward the South as the only way to bind up the wounds of the nation rapidly and permanently. Constantly he portrayed himself as the peaceful conciliator following in the footsteps of the beloved Lincoln. But Johnson foiled his image as a gentle peacemaker by assailing his opponents with a rash of intemperate and vicious personal attacks.

Campaigners for the Radical Republicans matched the president blow for blow, and they, too, were not averse to using sordid tactics. Often they deliberately stirred up war hatreds, which came to be known as "waving the bloody shirt." Again and again they reminded their listeners that the South had started the terrible carnage and suffering of the recent war, and they added that the Southerners still had not repented for their twin sins of slavery and secession.

The elections of 1866 resulted in a landslide victory for the Radical Republicans, who now felt they had received a mandate from the people to move ahead with a much stricter policy toward the South. Knowing they now had the votes to easily override any presidential vetoes, the Radicals passed the drastic Military Reconstruction Act of March 2, 1867, supplemented by three other tough measures. Into the ashcan went the southern state governments set up under the mild Johnson program. The former Confederacy, except for readmitted Tennessee, was divided into five military districts, each commanded by a general. These officers were instructed to form new governments in which blacks could vote and whites who had helped the Confederacy lost their suffrage. This meant that the majority of white southern men were denied the ballot.

To achieve readmission to the Union, the southern states now were required to call new conventions elected by universal manhood suffrage, ratify the Fourteenth Amendment, and guarantee in their state constitutions the right of black men to vote (this was superseded in 1870 by the Fifteenth Amendment). Congress reserved to itself the power to decide when to restore each state to the Union, end military rule, and accept that state's newly elected members of the House and Senate.

Clearly the Radical Republicans were now in the driver's seat, and they boldly tried to reduce both the executive and judicial branches of the government to positions inferior to Congress. They virtually deprived the president of his power as commander in chief by an act requiring that he issue all military orders through the chief general of the army, Ulysses S. Grant. Congress, fearful that peacetime military rule might be declared unconstitutional, took the unprecedented step of prohibiting appeals to the Supreme Court in any cases arising under the Reconstruction Acts of 1867. Then, to prevent Johnson from appointing justices to the Supreme Court, Congress decreed that whenever a justice died or resigned he was not to be replaced.

Intoxicated by power, the Radical Republicans had one last goal — to drive from office the president who had repeatedly tried to obstruct their policies. But they needed to find some legal charge on which he could be convicted in an impeachment trial. Since Johnson had not committed treason or bribery or broken a law, the Radicals decided they must create some new law that they strongly believed he would break, so they pushed through Congress the Tenure of Office Act. Contrary to a precedent established in Washington's administration (see page 14), this act required the president to obtain the consent of the Senate before he could dismiss any of his appointees who had previously been confirmed by that body.

The one member of his Cabinet whose conduct might compel Johnson to dismiss him was Secretary of War Edwin M. Stanton, a holdover from the Lincoln administration. Outwardly respectful toward the president, Stanton secretly was a spy and informer for the Radicals. When Johnson had sufficient evidence to prove Stanton's disloyalty, he wanted to remove him from his Cabinet.

The president felt secure about taking this action. In the first place, he was certain that the Tenure of Office Act was unconstitutional, and he was eager to have a test case in which the court would overturn it. Secondly, he believed that this trumped-up act could not apply to Stanton, since he had been given his office by Lincoln and was not Johnson's appointee.

So the president asked for Stanton's resignation, and when the secretary of war refused to step down, Johnson dismissed him. Then he quickly named Grant as the new secretary of war *ad interim*. Grant had agreed to take the job, but soon he changed his mind. The Radicals dangled in front of the general a promise to run him as the Republican presidential candidate in 1868, and Grant succumbed to the proposition, handing the Cabinet position back to Stanton. Johnson had been rebuffed, but he would not give up the fight. Again he dismissed Stanton and named Major General Lorenzo Thomas of Delaware to take his place. Stanton, goaded by the Radicals, refused to relinquish his post and barricaded himself in the War Department.

The Radical-dominated House of Representatives now moved swiftly to impeach the president for "high crimes and misdemeanors," which, according to the Constitution, are impeachable charges. Johnson was indicted on eleven counts, including such vague and transparent accusations as trying to bring disgrace and ridicule upon Congress. But the heart of the case against the president was that he had willfully violated the Tenure of Office Act.

Johnson failed in his effort to get an early court hearing on the constitutionality of the act he had defied, so he had to stand trial for impeachment before the Senate. The senators were the jurors, and each had a single vote. Supreme Court Chief Justice Salmon P. Chase presided over the historic proceedings.

The attention of the entire nation was riveted on the Senate chamber, where the president was being tried before a court that had the power to force him from office. The electrifying impeachment trial sparked such intense interest that visitors scrambled wildly for the thousand tickets to sit in the gallery.

Radicals in the House of Representatives, led by frail but zealous Thaddeus Stevens, argued the case for the prosecution. A battery of prominent lawyers defended the president. The trial continued for several weeks. First one side would make a major point; then the other side would counter with its own effective argument. Finally the testimony ended, followed by closing arguments from both sides. Then the senators decided to vote first on the eleventh article of impeachment, chiefly because the Radicals believed it had the best chance of succeeding. This article included the charge that the president had broken the Tenure of Office Act.

The defense was certain that all twelve Democratic senators would vote for acquittal. The prosecution felt confident that it could count on at least thirty-five Republicans to vote against the president. Just one more vote was needed by the Radicals to achieve the two-thirds majority required for conviction. There were seven other Republican senators who had not yet publicly declared how they stood. All seven needed to vote "not guilty" for the president to retain his office; the odds against this happening seemed immense. To make matters even worse for Johnson, near the end of the trial one of the uncommitted senators, James W. Grimes of Iowa, had suffered a stroke and was confined to his bed.

Ironically, all seven fence sitters were Radicals themselves who had consistently opposed Johnson's policies and disliked him personally. So the question in their minds was not whether they approved of the man in the White House. It was instead whether the president, regardless of his flaws and faults, had committed a crime for which he deserved to be forced out of office. Were their fellow Radicals intent on punishing Johnson for breaking the law, as they claimed, or for having political beliefs with which they disagreed?

Enormous pressure was brought to bear on the seven wavering senators. The president's defenders appealed to their sense of justice and fair play. Their Radical friends lectured them about loyalty to the cause and reminded them that the voters back home would hold them accountable if they supported a president who was grossly unpopular in most of the North and Midwest.

Nevertheless, the silent seven held their own counsel, and no one was certain how they would vote when the Senate began to ballot on May 16, 1868. But the hopes of the Radicals sagged when Senator Grimes, looking pale and weak, was carried by four men to his seat.

The roll call began, and each senator rose to his feet and called out his vote. Tension mounted every time one of the uncommitted senators announced his decision. One by one, all seven of the doubtful Radicals voted "not guilty." Even Senator Grimes struggled to his feet and cast his negative vote in a firm voice. The final count on the eleventh article of impeachment was 35–19 in favor of conviction—one vote short of the necessary two-thirds majority. President Johnson was acquitted also on the other ten counts.

By a single vote, Andrew Johnson was found not guilty in the most important trial in American history. He completed his term in the White House and then returned to his home in Tennessee. In 1875 he won election to the Senate and took the same seat he had left many years before when Tennessee seceded. Johnson thus became the only former president ever elected to the Senate, which, ironically, was the body that had almost ended his presidency.

But the seven Republican senators who had defied their party to vote for Johnson's acquittal were not so fortunate. Not one of them was ever reelected to the Senate, and some of these brave dissenters were treated like lepers by former friends and neighbors.

Even though they were renounced by their party and denounced by their constituents, the seven courageous Republicans performed a noble service to the nation by helping to set a precedent that the president cannot be removed from office simply because of his political views, no matter how unpopular or unorthodox they may be. Senator Lyman Trumbull of Illinois, one of the doubtful seven who voted for Johnson, put it this way: ". . . Once set, the example of impeaching a President for what, when the excitement of the hour shall have subsided, will be regarded as insufficient cause, no future President will be safe who happens to differ with a majority of the House and two-thirds of the Senate on any measure deemed by them important. . . . What then becomes of the checks and balances of the Constitution so carefully devised and so vital to its perpetuity? They are all gone."

Limiting the Scope of the Fourteenth Amendment

There was no doubt that the clause in the Fourteenth Amendment providing due process and equal protection would be used to protect blacks from unjust discrimination. But was it designed to protect other citizens besides blacks? Congressman John A. Bingham of Ohio, the amendment's chief author, said it was. Bingham knew that the Bill of Rights guarded the rights of citizens only against potential abuses by the federal government; he intended that the Fourteenth Amendment would extend this protection to similar abuses by the state governments. Addressing his House colleagues in 1871, three years after the Fourteenth Amendment had been ratified, Bingham asserted that it had been created to "vest in Congress a power to protect the rights of citizens against the States, and individuals in States, never before granted."

This extended meaning of the Fourteenth Amendment was first put to a court test in the *Slaughterhouse Cases* in 1873. They were based on a law that had been passed by the carpetbag Louisiana legislature, granting a monopoly in the slaughtering business in New Orleans to one company. The state justified the monopoly as a health measure.

By this law about one thousand New Orleans butchers were denied the right to work. Prior to the Fourteenth Amendment the outraged butchers would have brought suit against the monopoly in a state court. But now they took their case to a federal court, alleging that the Louisiana law had violated the Fourteenth Amendment in that it abridged their privileges and immunities, denied them equal protection of the laws, and deprived them of their property without due process of law.

When the case reached the Supreme Court, the majority of the justices were genuinely shocked by this new interpretation of the Fourteenth Amendment. They maintained that the purpose of the amendment was simply to protect the recently freed blacks from oppression by the whites in the South. By a 5-4 vote the Supreme Court ruled against the butchers, asserting that the rights guaranteed under the Fourteenth Amendment did not pertain to them.

This ruling came at a time when the Court was trying to lessen the control of the federal government over state affairs. During the Reconstruction era Congress had ruled supreme over the states, and the Court was intent on restoring the balance between state and federal power. In the *Slaughterhouse Cases* the majority of the justices held that there is a difference between being a citizen of the United States and being a citizen of a state, and the Fourteenth Amendment applies only to United States citizenship. Otherwise, the effect of this amendment would be to "fetter and degrade the State governments by subjecting them to the control of Congress."

The *Slaughterhouse Cases* heralded the revival of states' rights in the 1870s. But these cases also are significant because of the more forward-looking views of the dissenters. Justice Joseph P. Bradley, one of the four judges who voted to support the butchers, defied the majority opinion when he wrote, ". . . a law which prohibits a large class of citizens from adopting a lawful employment, or from following a lawful employment previously adopted, does deprive them of liberty as well as property without due process of law." According to his reading of the Fourteenth Amendment, Bradley concluded, "It is futile to argue that none but persons of the African race are intended to be benefited by this Amendment. They may have been the primary cause of the Amendment, but its language is general, embracing all citizens, and I think it was purposely so expressed."

Justice Noah Swayne, also writing in dissent, said that the Court had no authority to interpolate a limitation of the Fourteenth Amendment that was neither expressed nor implied. "Our duty is to execute the law," counseled Swayne, "not to make it. The protection provided was not intended to be confined to those of any particular race or class, but to embrace equally all races, classes and conditions of men."

Another dissenter, Justice Stephen J. Field, insisted that the Fourteenth Amendment protects "the citizens of the United States against the deprivation of their common rights by state legislation." In his judgment the amendment had been enacted "to place the common rights of American citizens under the protection of the national government."

The importance of the *Slaughterhouse Cases* in American history is that they set a judicial precedent whereby the protection of individual rights against state encroachments was delayed for more than half a century. Fifty-two years would pass before the Supreme Court reversed itself and held that at least portions of the Bill of Rights were applicable to the states by means of the Fourteenth Amendment. In *Gitlow* v. *New York* (1925) the Court, reviewing a case that involved freedom of speech and the press, made the landmark decision that these rights that ". . . are protected by the First Amendment from abridgment by Congress are among the fundamental personal rights and 'liberties' protected by the due process clause of the Fourteenth Amendment from impairment by the states."

In its decision on the *Slaughterhouse Cases*—by a one-vote margin—the Supreme Court apparently had killed the idea that the Fourteenth Amendment guarantees Americans' rights against possible state interference. But this was an idea that would not stay buried. *Gitlow* v. *New York* was just the opening salvo in a long, successful campaign to extend the Bill of Rights to protect individuals against injustices perpetrated by state governments.

President by a Single Vote

Many changes came to the vanquished South when Reconstruction was in the hands of the Radical Republicans. Federal troops were stationed throughout the devastated region. Many former Confederates were disfranchised, and at the same time large numbers of ex-slaves could troop to the polls. In five of the southern states more blacks could vote than whites.

State and local governments were dominated by three groups—carpetbaggers, scalawags, and blacks. The carpetbaggers were Northerners who, according to ex-Confederates, moved to the South with supposedly no more possessions than could be carried in a single carpetbag. Some of them were unscrupulous fortune hunters, while others were sincere, honest men who wanted to bring about better conditions in the South. Allied with these transplanted Northerners were some southern whites, sarcastically called scalawags, who were depicted as traitors by many former Confederates. The third group in the ruling triumvirate was the blacks. They won many seats in the state legislatures, and more than a dozen blacks were elected to Congress, including two senators.

Many of the men who had fought for the Confederacy still believed in white supremacy; they were embittered because their former slaves could vote and be elected to state and national offices. Some white Southerners organized secret terrorist societies, the most notorious of which was the Ku Klux Klan. Wearing white robes and hoods, the Klansmen would mount their horses and ride together at night, intimidating carpetbaggers, scalawags, and especially blacks. They would burn the houses and crops of blacks, often flog their victims, and sometimes even murder them. In one Louisiana parish, or county, the white-robed terrorists killed or wounded 200 blacks in two days. The Klan was often successful in preventing frightened blacks from exercising their political rights. White employers and landlords also pressured blacks to stay away from the polls by threatening to take away their jobs or evict them from their homes.

In spite of the deep-seated hatreds that plagued this era, the carpetbag governments in the southern states achieved some overdue reforms. They established free public school systems that were new to most of the South. Property rights were guaranteed to women. Taxation in some states was made more equitable. Public works were started, and the facilities to care for the poor and the mentally ill were improved.

On the other hand, some carpetbag officeholders were guilty of rampant graft and corruption. Votes in the state legislatures were sold to the highest bidders. Lucrative government contracts and rich public lands were bought by businessmen who slipped money under the table to corrupt officials. State legislatures paid ridiculously high sums for such "legislative supplies" as hams, champagne, bourbon, bonnets, suspenders, and corsets.

But during the Reconstruction period, while Ulysses S. Grant was

58 / By a Single Vote!

president, corruption was not limited to the South. It was prevalent in many parts of the nation, particularly in city governments, and the most outrageous example was Boss Tweed's ring in New York City. At the national level the Grant administration was riddled with graft. Grant's vice president, his secretary of war, his personal secretary, and even his own brother-in-law, along with several key members of Congress, were accused of financial misdeeds. While the president himself was not charged with dishonesty, he was portrayed as an inept administrator who coddled his crooked cronies. Some of his fellow Republicans were so disgusted and embarrassed by the unsavory conduct of Grant's colleagues that they refused to support the Civil War general for a second term in 1872. Calling themselves Liberal Republicans, they formed a separate party and voted for Horace Greeley, who ran for president on the tickets of both the Liberal Republican and Democratic parties.

Even though Greeley was defeated, the political pendulum began swinging back toward the Democrats for the first time since before the Civil War. The Democrats profited from the rift in the GOP between the Grant regulars and the reformers, and they also picked up support when the Panic of 1873 struck and voters tended to blame the Grant administration for the ensuing depression and unemployment. In 1874 the Democrats proved their comeback was authentic when they regained control of the House of Representatives.

As Grant's second term drew to a close, Republicans were deeply concerned by the strong resurgence of the Democratic party in the South. One by one, the southern states had been readmitted to the Union. Moreover, the Radical Republicans' fervor to protect the rights of the blacks was petering out. Southern whites moved back into a dominant position in one southern state after another, and by 1876 federal troops remained only in South Carolina, Louisiana, and Florida, the three states that had not yet been restored to complete home rule.

When the Republican convention assembled in Cincinnati in June, the party leaders knew they faced an uphill battle to hang onto the White House. Grant would have liked a third term, but the charges against his administration hung like an albatross around his neck. The Republican delegates were anxious to retire from office the unpopular president and give the nomination to someone else. The choice of many at the convention was House Speaker James G. Blaine of Maine. Blaine was a popular figure, but he had one serious drawback. His congressional career had been stained by alleged shady dealings with railroad interests, and reformers within the party wanted a standard-bearer who would not perpetuate the already embarrassing stigma of graft that Republicans had to deal with.

Nevertheless, Blaine had strong support in many delegations, and on the opening night of the convention his candidacy was boosted by a fiery nomination speech delivered by Colonel Robert G. Ingersoll, who rather ironically referred to the besmirched House Speaker as the "plumed knight." Ingersoll's emotional address touched off such an enthusiastic demonstration that Blaine's managers wanted the delegates to vote that night while the bandwagon for their candidate was still rolling at a frenzied pace.

But the plan for an early Blaine nomination was dashed by an unexpected, mysterious incident. Suddenly all the gas lights in the convention hall went out. The janitors discovered that the building's main gas pipe had been severed (perhaps by anti-Blaine delegates), and the convention had to be adjourned. By the next morning the euphoria over Blaine's nomination had subsided, and his opponents were able to put together a coalition that slowed his bandwagon.

Although the plumed knight led on the first six ballots, he failed to capture the 379 delegate votes needed for nomination. Finally, on the seventh ballot the convention ended the deadlock by giving the nomination to Governor Rutherford B. Hayes of Ohio, a dark-horse candidate who had received only 61 votes on the first ballot. Hayes was selected largely because he had acquired a reputation for honesty and moderation and had not alienated any of the party factions.

A Civil War officer who had been wounded five times in battle, Hayes had been commended by General Grant for conspicuous gallantry. While still in the army, he was elected to Congress in 1864, but he refused to leave his command until the war ended. Hayes took his seat in the House in December 1865 and was reelected in 1866. He made few speeches and took no part in the angry debates over Reconstruction but voted consistently with his party.

In 1867 and again in 1869 Hayes was elected governor of Ohio, and he proved to be an able, efficient administrator. After his second term in the statehouse, he retired briefly from politics but was persuaded in 1874 to run for Congress again. That was the year when the Democrats regained the House, and Hayes was one of the many Republicans who went down to defeat. But in 1875 he was elected to his third term as governor of Ohio, and when the Republicans picked him as their 1876 presidential candidate they knew they were running a man with a record that was solid and scandal-free, if not spectacular.

In an election year accented by graft and corruption, the Democrats also selected a presidential nominee known for his honesty and integrity, Governor Samuel J. Tilden of New York. As chairman of the state Democratic party Tilden had helped expose the criminal activities of Boss William Tweed; as governor he had crushed the crooked "Canal Ring," which had fed on graft from funds appropriated to rebuild state canals.

Tilden had strong credentials as a reformer, but he was not the typical back-slapping politician. A millionaire bachelor, Tilden was shy and retiring, coldly aloof, and very secretive, an austere intellectual who found no pleasure in mingling with the crowds at political rallies or swapping stories with a bevy of cronies.

The campaign began with the Democrats favored to capture the White House for the first time since the election of James Buchanan twenty years before. The Republicans had giant obstacles to overcome — the scandals of the Grant administration, the hard times following the Panic of 1873, and the corruption of the Republican-sponsored carpetbag governments in the South. But the GOP could still win votes by fanning the bitterness engendered by the Civil War. Colonel Ingersoll, remembered for his stirring convention speech for Blaine, stumped the country for Hayes, reminding voters that "not every Democrat was a rebel, but every rebel was a Democrat." Also, the white supremacists in South Carolina played into the Republicans' hands when they killed several blacks in a riot in July. Republicans charged that if the Democrats won the election, depraved Southerners again would ride high, intent on undoing Appomattox.

The South posed a troublesome question for Tilden: should he be elected, what reconstruction policies would he endorse? If he said he favored greater leniency toward white Southerners, he would lose the votes of many northern Democrats. If, on the other hand, he took a strong stand against white supremacy in the South, he would alienate many Democrats south of the Mason-Dixon Line. Tilden was an exceedingly cautious man who hated to make tough decisions. But on the issue of how the South should be treated, he felt compelled to make some commitment. Consequently, shortly before the election, Tilden publicly announced his firm opposition to compensating Southerners for the loss of slaves, the damage done to their property, and the debts that had been incurred during the Civil War.

This candid statement brought cheers from the northern wing of the Democratic party, but it caused Tilden's support in the South to sag badly. White Southerners probably would still vote for him in preference to Republican Hayes; now, however, they were more concerned about electing Democratic governors and legislators than a Democratic president. The lukewarm, indifferent support given to Tilden by whites in the South became a significant factor when victory or defeat in the close election finally focused on three southern states.

The first returns on election night pointed toward a narrow victory for Tilden. The New Yorker carried his own state, New Jersey, Connecticut, and Indiana, and while the returns from the South were still fragmentary, Tilden appeared to be sweeping that region handily. Democrats gathered in the streets of New York City, jubilantly celebrating their conquest of the White House, and soon after midnight Tilden himself announced his glorious triumph.

Meanwhile, Republicans across the land were filled with gloom and despair. Sadly Hayes acknowledged his defeat in his diary. The chairman of the GOP, Zachariah Chandler, went to bed convinced that his party had lost the presidency. Even most of the Republican newspapers conceded that Tilden had won the election.

Past midnight the editors of the *New York Times*, a staunchly Republican paper, were debating whether they, too, should say in their morning edition that Tilden had won the election. Their discussion was interrupted by a phone call from Democratic Senator William Barnum of Connecticut, who asked for the latest information about the election returns. He said he was particularly interested in the status of South Carolina, Florida, and Louisiana. Barnum was told that the vote count from these three states was still very small and inconclusive.

Following this phone conversation, John C. Reid, the avidly anti-Tilden managing editor of the *Times*, tallied the electoral votes already won by both candidates and then reached this startling conclusion — if Hayes could carry the three southern states that Barnum had asked about, he could win the election by one electoral vote! And since these three states were the only ones still under carpetbag control, there was at least a slim chance they could end up in Hayes's column.

Reid communicated this intriguing possibility to GOP headquarters, and soon the Republican officials in the three targeted states were telegraphed the same message: "Hayes is elected if we have carried South Carolina, Florida, and Louisiana. Can you hold your state? Answer immediately." Then Reid returned to his office to prepare the next edition of the *Times*, which blatantly proclaimed that "Hayes had 185 electoral votes and is elected."

The Democrats were surprised by the *Times*'s claim, and at first they gave it little credibility. After all, the Republicans had already conceded that Tilden had captured 184 electoral votes, only one vote short of the number needed to win. And Tilden's supporters believed that the three southern states that had not yet tallied their final returns would go Democratic, just as every other state in the South had done. But even if the Democrats did not take all three doubtful states, only one more state in Tilden's column would assure his victory. Louisiana seemed almost certain to put Tilden over the top; the Associated Press was reporting Democratic claims that he would carry the state by 20,000 votes.

Soon political chieftains from both parties, called "visiting statesmen" by the newspapers, were headed southward to investigate the confused situation. On November 10, three days after the election, President Grant ordered General William T. Sherman to alert his troops in the three southern states "to preserve peace and good order, and to see that the proper and legal Boards of Canvasses are unmolested in the performance of their duties." Then the president sent additional soldiers to Louisiana and Florida; there already was a large contingent of federal troops in South Carolina.

The canvassing boards in each state had the power to throw out irregular ballots, investigate charges of fraud, intimidation, and violence related to the election, and ultimately certify the official count of the legally cast popular vote. Since Republicans controlled these election boards, the Democrats feared that their rivals would try to distort the returns to their advantage.

Actually, both sides were guilty of unfair and illegal practices during this heated election. The Democrats resorted to intimidation and even violence to prevent blacks, who were predominantly Republican, from voting. Often they applied economic pressure on the blacks, threatening to take away their jobs or evict them from their rented houses if they appeared at the polls. Republican election boards retaliated by stuffing ballot boxes with large numbers of bogus votes for Hayes and eliminating enough Tilden votes on the meagerest of technicalities to guarantee a GOP victory.

Bribes were also dangled by the Democrats before the Republican-dominated canvassing boards. In Louisiana, for instance, it was alleged that if the vote counters would certify that their state had gone Democratic, they would receive a payment of $1,000,000 from the Democratic National Committee. When these offers were relayed to Tilden, he ordered that they be rescinded; the honest New Yorker refused to let anyone "buy" him the presidency.

In Florida, the only one of the disputed states with a majority of whites, a slim Tilden majority was wiped out by the election board. Hayes carried South Carolina by a narrow margin, but the Democrats elected a governor and carried the legislature. In Louisiana the most outrageous fraud occurred. The election board eliminated the votes of whole parishes in which there was any evidence that blacks might have been intimidated, thus switching a Tilden majority of about 3,500 votes into a Hayes victory. It is difficult to tell who would have won these three states in a fair election, but most historians have given the nod to Tilden in both Louisiana and Florida and to Hayes in South Carolina.

The Democrats, stunned and angered by the Republican shenanigans in the South, then devised another way that they thought could elect Tilden. The Republicans had carried Oregon, but one of the state's three electors was a postmaster, and the Constitution forbids federal officeholders from serving as an elector. So Oregon's Democratic governor replaced the postmaster with a Democratic elector and declared that Oregon was giving two electoral votes to Hayes and one to Tilden. The Democrats were jubilant, but their celebrations were premature because the postmaster resigned from his government job and claimed that he now could legally cast his ballot for Hayes.

The canvassing boards in all the disputed states forwarded to Washington certified returns saying that Hayes had captured their states. But Democratic leaders in each of these states sent in different sets of votes showing Tilden the winner. The Constitution provides that the electoral vote shall be counted by the president of the Senate and that if no candidate obtains a majority of the vote, the House of Representatives then elects the president. In 1876 the Senate was controlled by the Republicans, while the Democrats had a majority in the House. How could a Republican Senate and a Democratic House of Representatives agree on the twenty electoral votes that each party claimed?

A joint committee of the two houses discussed at length various suggestions for resolving the dilemma. Finally, the legislators decided to set up an electoral commission that would investigate the conflicting returns and then award the electoral votes, state by state, to the candidate with the best claim to them. This commission was to have the final authority in allocating the votes, unless both houses agreed to overrule its decisions.

There were to be fifteen members of the commission: five senators, five representatives, and five Supreme Court justices. Seven Republicans and seven Democrats would serve on the commission; the fifteenth member would be a Supreme Court justice chosen by the other four justices named to the commission. These other justices selected as the fifteenth member Justice David Davis, a Republican from Illinois who was widely respected for his independent judgment and fair decisions.

Democratic leaders felt that Davis would not be unduly influenced by partisan arguments and, on the strength of the evidence, would vote to give at least one of the disputed states (or the single disputed electoral vote in Oregon) to Tilden. But whatever high expectations the Democrats were harboring suddenly declined when news arrived that the Illinois legislature had elected Justice Davis to the Senate, which made him ineligible to serve on the electoral commission. The four other judges on the commission then chose Justice Joseph P. Bradley to take Davis's place. Although like Davis a Republican, Bradley appeared to be the most independent of the remaining members of the Court, and the Democrats hoped that he would not let politics interfere with his perception of the evidence.

After the electoral commission listened to the opposing arguments and discussed the facts that were presented, it appeared that seven Republican members wanted to give Hayes all the disputed votes and the seven Democrats intended to give them all to Tilden. Then Justice Bradley would have the awesome responsibility of casting the tie-breaking vote. In effect, one man was being cast in the unique, unimaginable role of selecting the president of the United States!

Florida was the first of the disputed states to be voted upon. On the night before the decision was to be handed down, a prominent Democrat, John G. Stevens, called at the home of Bradley, who was his personal friend. The Supreme Court justice read Stevens a statement in which he upheld the Democrats' claim that Florida's four electoral votes should go to Tilden. Stevens was overjoyed and immediately reported his good news to Democratic headquarters.

But the next morning Bradley did an incredible about-face and voted with the seven other Republicans to give Florida to Hayes. What had happened? No one knows for certain, but after Stevens left Bradley's house, the justice was visited past midnight by two Republicans: Senator Frederick T. Frelinghuysen of New Jersey and Secretary of the Navy George M. Robson. These stalwart Republicans must have convinced Bradley that the election of a Democratic president would result in a national calamity.

After the Florida decision, the electoral commission voted separately on the disputed votes of Louisiana, Oregon, and South Carolina. Each time the verdict was the same — Hayes was the winner — and each time by the same 8-7 majority. When the commission completed its work, it recommended to Congress that Hayes be elected with 185 electoral votes to Tilden's 184.

Throughout all sections of the country the Democrats screamed that they had been robbed. Their man had won the popular vote by over one quarter of a million votes (Tilden: 4,288,546: Hayes: 4,034,311). How could it be possible that he was not awarded at least one of the twenty disputed electoral votes? The *Cincinnati Enquirer,* a newspaper in Hayes's home state, denounced the election as "the monster fraud of the century." In the House of Representatives enraged Democrats forced through a resolution proclaiming that Tilden had been "duly elected President of the United States."

Then the die-hard Democrats proposed another tactic: they would stage a filibuster in Congress to delay the completion of the election count until after the day set for the inauguration of the new president. March 4, the day that the Constitution then required a presidential term to begin, was only a few days away. What would happen if March 4 arrived and no president was inaugurated? No one could say whether this grim possibility would shake the very foundations of our constitutional system.

An even more ominous fear gripped the nation — would a dreadful new civil war break out? Just one short decade after the horrible conflict that had torn North and South apart, there was an escalating danger of another violent confrontation, only this time it would pit Democrats against Republicans. In at least eleven states Democrats were forming "Tilden Minutemen" groups, gathering rifles, and angrily shouting "Tilden or Blood!" and "On to Washington!" Officers of state militias wrote to Tilden, offering to put armed battalions at his command. Irate Republicans responded that if the Democrats resorted to warfare, the party of Lincoln would give them a sound thrashing. President Grant, concerned that Democratic extremists might try to take Washington by storm, ordered more troops and artillery to protect the national capital.

The two men who were the principal actors in this pulsating drama were much calmer and more responsible than their rabid followers. Tilden refused to encourage resistance to the electoral commission's decision; he abhorred all the clamor to seize by force what he could not win by persuasion. Hayes, as president-elect, felt a strong obligation to do all that he could to end the turmoil.

Eight months before, when he had won the Republican nomination, Hayes had informed the southern white leaders that he favored ending the last vestiges of military reconstruction. While the electoral commission was deliberating, GOP chieftains were privately promising the Southerners that Hayes would honor his pledge. Besides removing the last federal troops from the South, the Republicans agreed that Hayes would appoint at least one Southerner to his Cabinet and support federal aid to education and internal improvements in the southern states. In return for these concessions, the Democrats promised to end their threat to delay the official election count past inauguration day.

So a bargain, known as the Compromise of 1877, had been struck. The controversial election count was finally completed in Congress on March 2. The next day Hayes took the oath of office in a private ceremony because March 4 fell on Sunday, and he was a devoutly religious man who would not transact business on the Sabbath. Actually, Hayes was much too good a man to be known in history by the derogatory nicknames he acquired from the 1876 presidential election—"His Fraudulency," "His Accidency," and "Old 8 to 7."

A Court Decision Leads to the Sixteenth Amendment

A federal tax on personal income was first levied during the Civil War. Needing additional sources of income for the expensive war effort, Congress in 1862 imposed a tax on individuals with annual incomes in excess of $600. Following the war, the personal exemption was raised to $1,000 in 1867 and then to $2,000. Two years later, in 1872, the income tax law expired.

Meanwhile, the income tax statute was being challenged in the courts as a violation of the constitutional requirement that direct taxes must be apportioned among the states according to population. (A direct tax is one that must be borne by the person upon whom it is levied; for example, the tax on land must be paid by the owner of that property.) But in 1881, when the case called *Springer* v. *United States* finally reached the Supreme Court, the Court rendered a unanimous decision that the income tax was not a direct tax, and, therefore, was constitutional.

There was no federal income tax in the United States for more than twenty years after the expiration of the first income tax law. Then, in the 1890s, when many people became concerned about the huge untaxed personal fortunes that were being made during this period of rapid industrialization, widespread pressure was generated for a revival of the income tax. Following the Panic of 1893 that was accompanied by a severe depression, funds in the Treasury shrank, and Congress in 1894 once again enacted an income tax law.

This time the courts were immediately barraged by attacks on the income tax. A test case was established in which a stockholder sued a corporation to prevent payment of an income tax on the proceeds from his stock.

The Supreme Court justices disagreed on the verdict in this case. Chief Justice Melville W. Fuller wrote: ". . . the Constitution prohibits any direct tax, unless in proportion to numbers as ascertained by the census; . . . is it not an evasion of that prohibition to hold that a general unapportioned tax, imposed upon all property owners . . . is not direct, in the meaning of the Constitution, because confined to the income therefrom?"

While Chief Justice Fuller's opinion certainly followed the letter of the law, his colleague, Justice John Marshall Harlan, took a much broader view. Justice Harlan stated that outlawing the income tax ". . . strikes at the very foundation of national authority in that it denies to the general government a power which is, or may become, vital to the very existence and preservation of the Union in a national emergency, such as that of war with a great commercial nation, during which the collection of all duties upon imports will cease or be materially diminished. . . . I cannot assent to an interpretation of the Constitution that impairs and cripples the just powers of the National Government in the essential matter of taxation, and at the same time discriminates against the greater part of the people of our country."

When the Court handed down its decision in this important 1895 case, called *Pollock* v. *Farmers' Loan and Trust Company*, five justices voted that the income tax law was unconstitutional and four justices voted to uphold it. Thus, by a one-vote margin the income tax was obliterated.

Nevertheless, pressure continued to mount for the restoration of the income tax as a large untapped source of future federal revenue and as a progressive form of taxation based on the equitable principle that persons who earn higher incomes would pay higher taxes. But since the Supreme Court had ruled that an income tax was unconstitutional, the only way it could be legalized was by adding a new amendment to the Constitution.

Because of strong opposition from powerful financial interests, Congress was in no hurry to accept an income tax amendment. Finally, in 1909, fourteen years after the Supreme Court invalidated the income tax, the Sixteenth Amendment empowering Congress to levy such a tax was approved by the Senate and the House of Representatives. The battle for ratification consumed another four years, but in 1913 the amendment went into effect after being ratified by the necessary three-fourths of the states.

At first taxes were collected only from single persons earning more than $3,000 a year and from married couples with an income of more than $4,000. Rates were set at 1 percent of income for the less affluent taxpayers, and even the wealthiest individuals paid Uncle Sam only 6 percent of their earnings. The first year's returns came to just $28 million.

The average family in 1914 felt nothing more than a pin prick from the national government when the income tax was collected. Ah, those were the days when a dollar earned meant 99 cents in the earner's pocket.

You Can Unscramble Eggs

When Theodore Roosevelt unexpectedly assumed the presidency in September 1901, following the assassination of William McKinley, Wall Street trembled. As governor of New York, outspoken TR had favored higher taxation, government regulation of corporations, and the protection of labor's rights. Because of Roosevelt's penchant for reform, political bosses in New York had helped maneuver him out of the statehouse and into the vice presidency, a powerless position where they figured he could cause no mischief. But due to the untimely death of conservative McKinley, that "damned cowboy," as Mark Hanna had described Roosevelt, had been propelled into the White House.

Soon after taking office, our youngest president (42) rolled up his sleeves, ready to do battle with anyone or anything that he felt was betraying the public interest. His first target was a mammoth, powerful railroad corporation, the Northern Securities Company. This corporation had evolved from a struggle between two railroad tycoons, Edward H. Harriman, the principal owner of the Union Pacific and Southern Pacific lines, and James J. Hill, the chief stockholder of the Great Northern and Northern Pacific railways. Both Harriman and Hill wanted to win control of the Burlington Railroad, thus securing a route to Chicago. When Hill put up some of his stock in Northern Pacific to purchase control of the Burlington, Harriman fought back and tried to buy enough of the Northern Pacific's shares to give him ownership of both lines.

Suddenly the price of Northern Pacific stock soared from $100 a share to $1,000, precipitating a Wall Street panic. As that stock zoomed upward, others fell with frightening rapidity. Standard Oil, for example, dropped 150 points. Stockbrokers feared that the entire market was in danger of imminent collapse.

At this point the imperial lord of finance, J. P. Morgan, offered a way out of the dilemma. Morgan, who was personally involved because he had invested heavily in Hill's railroads, proposed the formation of a giant holding company, capitalized at about $400 million, that would put the Great Northern, Northern Pacific, and Burlington railroads all under one control. An agreement was reached with Morgan, Hill, and Harriman all receiving shares and taking seats on the board of the new Northern Securities Company. Since Harriman already owned the major interest in two other western transcontinental railroads, it was obvious that a small clique of rail barons had a stranglehold on the routes that linked the West to the rest of the country. With no more competition, they could now charge railroad users whatever they pleased.

Public outrage over the creation of this new powerful monopoly gathered steam. Seizing upon this popular issue, President Roosevelt, in February 1902, directed Attorney General Philander C. Knox to prosecute the Northern Securities Company for violation of the Sherman Antitrust Act. This act had been almost wholly neglected since its passage in 1890, except for its use against labor unions to break up strikes that judges considered "in restraint of trade." But the original intent of the Sherman Antitrust Act was to prevent the organization and operation of trusts, and although the Northern Securities Company was called a holding company, Roosevelt believed it had all the monopolistic trappings of a trust and was subject to dissolution.

Shortly after the president announced his bold stand, J. P. Morgan visited him in the White House. Morgan and Roosevelt had long been friends, and the financier hoped he could coax the president to change his mind. Anxious to abort the pending lawsuit, Morgan said casually, "If we have done anything wrong, send your man [the attorney general] to my man [Morgan's lawyer], and they can fix it up."

Roosevelt replied that this was impossible. "I do not intend to fix it up," he said sternly, "but to stop it."

Morgan then tried to convince the president that the interests of the accused railroad companies were so tightly interwoven that it would not be feasible to break them up. "How can you unscramble eggs?" he smugly asked. It would not be easy, Roosevelt agreed, but this kind of difficult challenge invigorated the restless Roughrider in the White House.

By his action, Roosevelt antagonized many captains of finance and industry, but he won the plaudits of large segments of the population. In the summer, after his attorney general had started the lawsuit, the president made a speaking tour of the country. At one stop after another, he reiterated his belief that there should be no one in the nation so powerful or wealthy as to be above the law and that he intended to enforce it, no matter whose sacred cow he might be goring. Time and time again the crowds were enthralled by Roosevelt's fighting words, and they cheered him wildly as a towering champion of reform.

It took two years for the courts to unscramble the Northern Securities case. Eventually, in March 1904, the Supreme Court by the narrowest of margins — 5 to 4 — ordered the holding company dissolved. Theodore Roosevelt's reputation as a trustbuster was made, and through all the subsequent years of our history he alone has borne this title, even though his White House successor, William Howard Taft, waged twice as many successful antitrust suits in four years as Roosevelt had done in seven.

One jarring note dampened Roosevelt's jubilation when the Supreme Court announced its significant decision in the Northern Securities case. Oliver Wendell Holmes, whom Roosevelt had recently named to the Court because he was known as a crusading progressive, had voted with the minority that favored the holding company. Roosevelt was livid when he learned that his own appointee had deserted the trustbusting cause. "I could carve out of a banana," the president stormed, "a judge with more backbone than that!"

Reforming the Election of Senators

At about the same time that Theodore Roosevelt was launching his career as a trustbuster, other progressive reforms were mushrooming across the country. The first decade of the twentieth century saw the rapid spread of the initiative, referendum, and recall. The direct primary was another new democratic practice; it took the nomination of candidates away from boss-ridden party conventions and gave it to the voters in a preliminary election held before the final election.

Progressive crusaders also wanted to reform the method of electing United States senators, but this could be accomplished only by amending the Constitution. When the Founding Fathers created the Senate, they made it much further removed from the people than was the House of Representatives. While the members of the lower house were to be elected every two years directly by the people, the members of the upper house were to be elected to six-year terms by their state legislatures. Throughout the entire nineteenth century and into the second decade of the twentieth century this method of selecting senators persisted; such towering giants of the Senate as Daniel Webster, Henry Clay, and Thomas Hart Benton never were elected to their seats by the people.

Since they were beholden to state legislatures for their positions, senators often were the tools of political machines. This became a national concern in the graft-ridden period following the Civil War. Newspapers frequently carried sensational stories about the corruption prevalent in the upper house of Congress. The reformers' response to these scandals was to demand that senators be made responsible to the people instead of to state legislatures that too often selected senators they could control.

Another problem also stemmed from state legislatures electing senators. If one party controlled one branch of the state legislature and another party the other branch, balloting for a senator could continue indefinitely, causing a lengthy stalemate. If the deadlock could not be broken, the state was deprived of its full representation in the Senate. Between 1891 and 1905 fourteen Senate seats were left vacant by deadlocked state legislatures.

Many times individual congressmen introduced resolutions calling for a constitutional amendment to elect senators by popular vote, but again and again their resolutions died in committee. A large number of senators were in no rush to establish a new electoral method that might cause them to be turned out of office if the voters could decide their fate. By 1912 a total of 287 congressional resolutions for the direct election of senators had been introduced, but without success.

But the demand for reform was too pervasive and persistent to allow the issue to be permanently pigeonholed. Direct election of senators was a plank in the Populist party platform at every election, starting in 1892, and in the Democratic party platform in each presidential election from 1900 to 1912. State legislatures, beginning in 1894, petitioned Congress for a direct election amendment, and by 1905 the legislatures in thirty-one states had taken this step.

The House of Representatives bent to the will of the people. Between

1892 and 1902 an amendment resolution was passed five times in the House with only slight opposition. In 1900, when the House voted 240-15 in favor of an amendment to elect senators by popular vote, the measure was carried by a majority of representatives from every state except Connecticut and Maine. Still the Senate refused to act.

Frustrated by the Senate's obstinacy, the people of Oregon took the matter into their own hands. By initiative petition they established, in 1904, a law that called for the voters of each party to indicate their choice for a Senate seat in a primary election. Before this election every candidate for the state legislature had to sign one of two statements: the first statement pledged the candidate to vote for the people's choice for senator; the second statement allowed the candidate to disregard the people's choice. Most candidates for the state legislature, fearful of the voters' wrath, promised to vote for whomever the people wanted.

Other states followed Oregon's lead. By 1911 the Senate contained fourteen members who in effect had been elected by popular vote from states using variations of the so-called Oregon system. Moreover, some senators who previously opposed popular elections changed their minds when a grassroots campaign developed to call for a new constitutional convention unless Congress approved the disputed amendment. Fearful that a second constitutional convention might exceed its original purpose and make other sweeping changes in the Constitution, leaders in the Senate persuaded many of their colleagues that a new method of electing senators was certainly preferable to a new Constitution.

By 1911 the situation seemed ripe for the passage of the Seventeenth Amendment by both houses of Congress. But the amendment that easily won approval of the necessary two-thirds majority in the House of Representatives contained a clause that gave the states exclusive power to set the time, place, and manner of senatorial elections. This state enforcement clause caused a serious rift in the Senate. The progressive senators wanted to delete the clause and let the federal government have the authority to regulate the election of senators. But many southern senators, remembering the excessive power exerted by the national government during the Reconstruction period, said they could not support the Seventeenth Amendment unless it specifically denied the federal government the right to regulate senatorial elections.

First the Senate balloted on this controversial clause. Progressives and Southerners competed to win over uncommitted senators, and both sides predicted a close vote. When the count was taken, the proposal to eliminate the state enforcement clause tied, with forty-four senators voting yes and the same number voting no. Vice President James S. Sherman, a New York Republican, cast the tie-breaking vote in favor of deleting the contested clause, thus giving the federal government the power to determine the manner in which senators would be elected.

With this obstacle out of the way, the Senate approved the constitutional amendment, 64-24. At the next session of Congress the House accepted the Senate version by an overwhelming vote of 238-39. The measure was quickly ratified by three-fourths of the states, and on May 31, 1913, the Seventeenth Amendment went into effect. The Sixty-sixth Congress (1919–21) was the first in which all the senators had been selected by popular elections.

Did the voters throw out most of the senators who had been originally elected by state legislatures? No. Of the ninety-six senators who held office in 1919, fifty-six had been initially chosen by legislatures and then reelected by the people of their states.

Women Fight for the Ballot

The most sought-after goal of the reform movement that prodded the public conscience in the early part of the twentieth century was women's suffrage. But this crowning achievement was not attained without a long, arduous struggle.

The first organized push for women's suffrage began with the 1848 convention for women's rights led by Elizabeth Cady Stanton at Seneca Falls, New York. At that time nearly all adult white men had gained the right to vote, but in no state had women won any active role in political affairs. Women could not serve on juries or hold public office, and even their property passed to their husbands when they married. A wife was expected to stay inside her home and be totally subordinate to the will of her husband. According to one nineteenth-century male chauvinist, "A woman's name should appear in print but twice — when she marries and when she dies."

What reasons did men give for not extending the vote and other political rights to women? Some men claimed that women were intellectually inferior or that voting should be based on the capacity to perform military service. One flimsy excuse was that if women studied political issues and went to the ballot box, they would divert too much time and attention from their homemaking duties. Many members of Congress refused to picture women in any other role than an obedient wife and loving mother. "For my part when I go to my home," said Senator George Vest of Missouri during a women's suffrage debate in 1887, ". . . I want to go back, not to the embrace of some female ward politician, but to the earnest loving look and touch of a true woman. I want to go back to the jurisdiction of the wife, the mother; and instead of a lecture upon finance or the tariff, or upon the construction of the Constitution, I want those blessed loving details of domestic life and domestic love."

The first constitutional amendment calling for women's suffrage was introduced into Congress in 1868. Early efforts to secure the vote for women were enmeshed with the drive to enfranchise black males. When the Fifteenth Amendment in 1870 gave black men the vote, women agitated for suffrage particularly in the South, arguing that it would counterbalance the new black vote. But southern members of Congress, with their longstanding devotion to states' rights and their traditional belief in a genteel way of life, were the strongest opponents of women's suffrage. "Pitchfork Ben" Tillman, a prominent South Carolina senator, expressed the South's position when he declared that giving women the ballot would "mar the beauty and dim the luster of the glorious womanhood with which we have been familiar."

Even though supporters of a constitutional amendment reintroduced it at every session of Congress for half a century, women suffragists realistically agreed that the likeliest place for their cause to succeed was in the democratic West, rather than in the conservative Congress. The first region to give women the vote was the territory of Wyoming in 1869; the next year the Utah territory followed Wyoming's lead. When Wyoming gained statehood in 1890, it became the first state to enfranchise women. In 1893 Colorado let women vote, followed in 1896 by Utah and Idaho. A major advance occurred when the Progressive party, a vociferous proponent of women's suffrage, won a series of state referenda: in Washington (1910); California (1911); and Arizona, Kansas, and Oregon (1912). All of these early victories for women's suffrage were in rural states west of the Mississippi River.

The first industrial midwestern state to join the movement was Illinois in 1913, but here the women's vote was restricted to presidential and municipal elections. In this same year Woodrow Wilson became president. To make the incoming president fully aware of their crusade, five thousand women marched in Washington the day before Wilson's inauguration.

The peaceful parade almost turned into a disastrous riot. Police had granted a permit for the parade, but they did little to protect the determined women when angry men began attacking the marchers. The women had to fight their way from the start and took more than an hour to advance the first several blocks. They were spat upon, shoved, slapped, tripped, and sometimes knocked to the ground. Their banners were mutilated, their hats were pulled off, and their clothing was torn. Many of them were in tears from the assaults and the insults screamed by male chauvinists who lined the route. The women were able to complete their march only after cavalry troops from nearby Fort Myers were rushed into Washington to subdue the mob and restore order.

This ugly incident captured newspaper headlines and signaled the start of a militant new drive for a constitutional amendment. Parades and mass meetings proclaimed the cause of women's suffrage in cities and towns from Maine to Oregon. Thousands of letters, telegrams, and resolutions deluged senators and representatives. Huge delegations of women trooped to Washington to plead their case before members of Congress and a wary President Wilson, who favored states' rights and was dubious about supporting action at the national level.

The momentum for women's suffrage was steadily growing, but victory was not yet in sight. On March 17, 1914, the Senate voted for the first time on the suffrage amendment. The measure carried by a 35-34 vote, but this one-vote margin was far short of the two-thirds majority needed to adopt a constitutional amendment. The House first voted on the amendment on January 12, 1915, and it was defeated by thirty votes, 204-174.

When the United States entered World War I in 1917, effective new arguments were added to the women's arsenal. Hundreds of thousands of women were abandoning their aprons to work in industries that had lost much of their male labor force to the armed forces. Suffragists contended that if women could hold men's jobs, they were also entitled to equal rights at the polls. And they added that if World War I was the war to "make the world safe for democracy," as Wilson had proclaimed, then democracy should begin at home with women's suffrage.

These arguments finally won over the wavering Wilson, who announced his long-delayed support for the suffrage amendment on January 8, 1918. The next day the House of Representatives was scheduled to vote on the measure. Careful tallying by the suffrage groups showed that the vote would be extremely close and no one could foretell the outcome. Four of the amendment's supporters were ill, and it was doubtful whether they would be present for the House vote. Another advocate of women's rights might miss the vote because his wife was dying.

When the crucial House vote was taken, Representative Thetus Sims, a Tennessee Democrat, was in excruciating pain because he refused to have a broken arm and shoulder set until after he had voted in favor of women's suffrage. Republican House Leader James Mann of Illinois, who had been in a Baltimore hospital for six months, was so feeble that he could hardly stand upright, but he returned to the House to have his affirmative vote recorded. Congressman Henry Barnhart, a Democrat from Indiana, had to be carried into the House on a stretcher in order to vote for the amendment. The fourth ailing congressman, Democrat Robert Crosser of Ohio, also added his ballot to the women's cause. And Republican Representative Frederick Hicks of New York honored a pledge he had made to his wife, an ardent suffragist, and left her deathbed to answer the House roll call.

The votes of these five courageous men were needed to pass the suffrage amendment, which carried, 274 to 136. If a single member of the House who voted for the measure had switched to the negative side, the amendment would have fallen one vote short of the necessary two-thirds majority. Some of the suffragists in the House gallery cheered and others wept for joy; they believed their torturous crusade was nearly won.

The Senate, however, was not ready to fulfill the women's great dream. Senators who opposed the suffrage amendment no longer preached about preserving femininity and the family hearth, but they united solidly behind the theme that each state must decide for itself which of its citizens could vote. This states' rights argument was formidable, and it drew together not only a majority of southern senators, but also powerful well-known legislators from other sections of the country.

President Wilson, himself an adherent of states' rights before his recent conversion, decided to make a direct appeal to the Senate while it was debating the issue in October 1918. In an unprecedented visit to the upper house, the president interrupted the heated debate to stress the crucial role that women were playing in the war effort. "We have made partners of the women in this war," Wilson declared. "Shall we admit them only to a partnership of suffering and sacrifice and toil and not to a partnership of privilege and right? This war could not have been fought, either by the other nations engaged or by America, if it had not been for the services of the women. . . . I tell you plainly that this measure which I urge upon you is vital to the winning of the war."

In spite of the president's eloquent and patriotic remarks, the Senate defeated the amendment, 62 in favor to 34 opposed, just two votes short of the required two-thirds majority. Again, in February 1919, the Senate turned it down, this time by only one vote. But the tide was now running strongly in favor of the suffragists; in November 1918, more prosuffrage candidates had been elected to both houses of Congress.

President Wilson summoned the Sixty-sixth Congress to meet in special session on May 19, 1919, and once again he urged passage of the women's suffrage amendment. The newly elected members of Congress now were seated, and most of them threw their weight behind the amendment. On May 21 it was repassed by the House, this time by a whopping majority of 304 to 89. About two weeks later, on June 4, the Senate approved the measure by a 56-25 vote.

Even then there was a lingering doubt. Some members of Congress privately admitted they had voted for the suffrage amendment because they would have offended a large bloc of constituents by being counted in the enemy camp, but they confidently predicted that it would not be ratified by the necessary three-fourths of the states. They felt that at least thirteen states would reject the controversial measure.

By August 1919, fourteen states had ratified the amendment, but then the movement slowed. Month after month the battle raged, first in one state, then in another. Some state legislatures decided to defer action; others voted down the amendment. But the number of states that approved women's suffrage slowly increased. By the summer of 1920 thirty-five states had ratified, and the eyes of the nation then riveted on Tennessee, which could become the state that put the Nineteenth Amendment into operation.

The governor of Tennessee was reluctant to call a special session of the state legislature because Tennessee's constitution contained a provision to forestall ratification of constitutional amendments unless a state "convention or General Assembly shall have been elected after such amendment is submitted." However, in a related situation in Ohio, the Supreme Court ruled in June 1920 that referenda on constitutional amendments were invalid and unnecessary. So President Wilson wired the Tennessee governor that "it would be a real service to the party and to the nation if it is possible for you under the peculiar provision of your State Constitution, having in mind the recent decision of the Supreme Court in the Ohio case, to call a special session of the Legislature to consider the Suffrage Amendment. Allow me to urge this very earnestly."

The governor finally yielded, and on August 26, 1920 — about nine weeks before the next presidential election — Tennessee became the thirty-sixth state to ratify the amendment giving women the vote. Seventy-two years had passed since Elizabeth Cady Stanton and her allies had first inspired women to work for a cause that seemed so fair and just. Through tenacious persistence and dogged determination the mission finally succeeded.

The Invisible Empire Escapes Condemnation

In 1920, millions of women trooped to the polls for the first time in a presidential election, and they helped select an affable, handsome Republican, Warren G. Harding. Backslapping cordiality and loyalty to his party had propelled this small-newspaper publisher from Marion, Ohio, all the way to the White House, but these were not the qualities needed to produce an effective chief executive. Harding proved to be a woefully inept president, partly because he could not come to grips with the nation's thorniest problems and partly because he was cruelly deceived by the men in whom he had placed his trust. The Harding administration was caught in a whirlpool of corruption, including the notorious transfer of naval oil reserves at Teapot Dome, Wyoming, and Elk Hills, California, to greedy oil barons. When the president discovered the crimes that several high government officials had committed behind his back, he was stunned and desolate, but a fatal heart attack in the summer of 1923 spared him further agony.

Straitlaced, tight-lipped Vice President Calvin Coolidge then ascended to the presidency. With a reputation for unquestionable honesty, Coolidge quickly cleaned house, firing Harding's cronies of dubious integrity (including Attorney General Harry M. Daugherty) and ordering the wheels of justice to grind against those who had defrauded the government (including Secretary of the Interior Albert B. Fall).

With prosperity reigning and strong endorsements from business leaders, Coolidge had no difficulty winning the Republican presidential nomination in 1924. But the recent revelations of corruption in high GOP circles had disgusted the public, and these scandals should have boosted the Democrats' chances in 1924, just as Watergate did a half century later.

The Democrats, however, muffed this golden opportunity. Instead of uniting to capitalize on GOP misdeeds, they split into two warring groups. Consequently, their 1924 convention in New York City's Madison Square Garden produced probably the most acrimonious, fiercely contested battle in the history of political conventions. (The 1968 Democratic convention in Chicago was accompanied by ugly rioting and police brutality, but most of the unsavory behavior occurred outside the convention hall.) Moreover, the 1924 Democratic convention, held during an intense heat wave, was the longest in American history. From the opening gavel on June 24 through final adjournment on July 10, it spanned seventeen sweltering days. There were so many candidates for the presidential nomination — nineteen in all — that, in the interest of saving time, the nominating speeches were made before the adoption of the platform, and voting on the nominees was postponed until after the platform had been accepted. This reversal in the order of convention business not only broke with tradition but it also heightened the tension between the two combative factions.

In 1924 rural America was pitted against urban America in a titanic struggle for political domination. The chief Democratic candidate of the rural faction was William Gibbs McAdoo of California, Woodrow Wilson's secretary of the treasury and son-in-law. McAdoo, a Protestant, supported Prohibition, which was then in effect, and he did not take a strong stand against the Ku Klux Klan, which was riding a wave of popularity in the mid-1920s. His major rival was Alfred E. Smith of New York, a Catholic from poor Irish immigrant stock. Through determination and perseverance Smith had risen from working in a lowly job at a fish market in New York City to the governor's chair in the nation's most populous state. The leading spokesman of the urban wing of the Democratic party, Smith derided nationwide Prohibition as a failure and lashed out at the bigotry of the Ku Klux Klan.

Another strong opponent of the Klan was Senator Oscar W. Underwood of Alabama. When his fellow Alabaman, Forney Johnson, rose to place Underwood's name in nomination, he urged the convention to repudiate secret un-American organizations. Then Johnson assailed the Klan by name, which prompted a frenzied demonstration by the anti-Klan forces. Delegates, mainly from urban areas, scrambled out of their seats and poured into the aisles. The ardent marchers tried to wrest state banners from the grimly silent rural delegates, and fistfights erupted in the Colorado and Missouri delegations. Parading Democrats taunted their rivals with shouts of "Get up, you Kleagles," insinuating that all who stayed seated were card-carrying Klan members. For nearly half an hour the uproar continued, until finally the band restored order by playing "America, the Beautiful."

Those who squirmed uneasily in their chairs during the parade for Underwood had their raucous revenge when McAdoo's name was placed in nomination. Staging their own spirited demonstration, the supporters of McAdoo and Prohibition crowded the aisles and chanted derisively, "Booze! Booze! Booze!" (only to be answered by cries of "Ku, Ku, McAdoo!").

But the loudest and most prolonged cheering greeted Franklin D. Roosevelt's nomination of the "hometown boy," Al Smith. When

Roosevelt called Smith the "happy warrior," a wave of unrestrained exuberance swept through the ranks of urban delegates. They were so boisterous and difficult to tame that at one point a serious effort was made to adjourn the convention and move the proceedings to a more neutral site.

These wild, out-of-hand demonstrations when the presidential nominations were made set the stage for a bitter, prolonged fight over the platform plank involving the secret invisible empire known as the Ku Klux Klan. In the period following the Civil War the Klan had been composed chiefly of whites in the South intent on intimidating the blacks and keeping these newly freed ex-slaves in an inferior position. Its energies dissipated after Reconstruction when the whites regained control in the land of cotton. But the Klan was revived in 1915, and this new version of the hooded hatemongers had more targets, a wider base of operations, and greater influence at the national level. In addition to persecuting blacks, the resurgent Klan spewed out its venom at Catholics, Jews, and recent immigrants, and its base of operations spread from the South to many parts of the Midwest and West. At the 1924 Democratic convention the KKK was a power to be reckoned with, since it exerted an almost hypnotic influence over a large bloc of rural delegates.

After four days of wrangling heightened by raging tantrums from both sides, the platform committee finally decided to sidestep the divisive KKK issue. Instead of advocating a powerful anti-Klan statement, the majority report proposed an innocuous plank decrying all efforts to limit constitutional liberties. This tepid plank infuriated the enemies of the invisible empire, who then offered a minority plank condemning the Klan by name.

The heated, prolonged fight over these competing planks pushed the convention to the brink of chaos. Hundreds of additional police had to be summoned to Madison Square Garden to prevent physical violence. The aging William Jennings Bryan, three times the Democrats' presidential nominee and now one of the party's elder statesmen, stepped to the podium and begged the delegates not to let this single issue tear the party apart. In the interest of conciliation Bryan urged that the "three little words"—Ku Klux Klan—be left out of the platform. But Bryan's olive-branch plea was loudly booed by delegates who detested the hooded legions.

After painful hours of hostile exchanges, the delegates finally voted on the minority plank to repudiate the Ku Klux Klan as a vicious un-American institution. In one of the closest votes in convention history, the minority plank was defeated, $543^{3}/_{20}$ to $542^{7}/_{10}$. By less than one full vote the Democrats stopped short of defying the KKK by name. The vote closely followed factional lines, with most rural delegates opposing the minority plank and most urban delegates approving it.

The rancor over the Klan continued when the delegates balloted to select their presidential nominee. Neither McAdoo nor Smith could acquire the two-thirds vote necessary for nomination, but both men kept trying, ballot after ballot, day after day. Not until the record-setting 103d ballot, when the delegates had reached the point of utter exhaustion, did the convention abandon both front runners and give the nomination to a lackluster compromise candidate with moderate views. He was John W. Davis of West Virginia, a Wall Street lawyer who had served as Wilson's solicitor-general and ambassador to Britain.

The badly divided Democrats were incapable of working together in the fall campaign. Davis won less than 29 percent of the popular vote, and he carried only the South (including Oklahoma). The entire North and West supported Coolidge, who breezed to victory with an impressive 54 percent of the popular vote. A third-party candidate, Progressive Robert M. LaFollette, won his home state of Wisconsin and ran second to Coolidge in eleven western states.

After 1924 the popularity of the Ku Klux Klan declined sharply. The invisible empire, riddled by reports of crime and scandal in its top echelons, lost many adherents, and it was no longer a flaming issue by the time that the Democratic convention assembled in 1928. In that year the urban wing of the party clearly emerged as the dominant faction; on the first ballot the Democrats handed their presidential nomination to the favorite son of the teeming masses, happy warrior Al Smith.

The Vice President Is Asleep at the Switch

One of the few exciting episodes in the Coolidge administration involved the president's appointment of a Cabinet officer. Fresh from his 1924 election victory that he regarded as an impressive personal triumph, President Coolidge sent to the Senate the nomination of Charles B. Warren, a prominent Michigan attorney, to be his attorney general. The president anticipated little opposition to his appointment.

The nomination was favorably reported by the Committee on the Judiciary, but trouble developed when it reached the Senate floor. Various senators spoke in opposition to Warren, attacking his association with the monopolistic "Sugar Trust." Such a man, his opponents claimed, could not be relied upon to enforce the country's antitrust laws.

When it became evident that a close vote on the nomination was likely to result, an urgent call was sent out for Vice President Charles G. Dawes, whose vote might be needed in case of a tie. But Dawes was not to be found in his office or the Senate dining room.

The vice president, having been assured earlier by Senate leaders that only routine business was to be conducted that day, had slipped away from the Capitol to take a nap in his room at the Willard Hotel. While Dawes snoozed, the Senate voted 40-40 on the Warren nomination. Had the vice president been present, his single vote would have changed Warren's fate from rejection to confirmation.

As a last resort, a Republican senator changed his vote from aye to nay so that he could call for a reconsideration, which was a parliamentary maneuver to stall for time until the vice president (who had been located at his hotel) could reach the Capitol. Objecting to this tactical ploy, one of Warren's opponents moved to have the reconsideration of the appointment laid on the table. While the roll was being called on this latter motion, Dawes entered the chamber. But his mad dash to the Capitol was unrewarded; by a 41-39 vote the reconsideration of the Warren appointment was tabled and thus effectively killed.

President Coolidge was furious when he learned of the Senate's action. Not since 1868, when a partisan Senate dominated by Radical Republicans had turned down President Andrew Johnson's appointment of Henry Stanbery as his attorney general, had the upper house of Congress rejected a Cabinet nomination. Coolidge angrily renominated Warren, and while the Senate debate was in progress he sternly announced that if the legislators still refused to confirm Warren he would offer him a recess appointment. Then he scolded the Senate, declaring that he "hoped that the unbroken practice of three generations of permitting the President to choose his own Cabinet will not be changed . . . and that the President may be unhampered in choosing his own methods of executing the laws."

This arrogant stand by Coolidge provoked a storm of criticism in the Senate, whose members felt that their constitutional powers were endangered by a president who intended to give a rejected nominee a recess appointment. Several senators who had previously supported Warren now switched sides to punish the president for tampering with their prerogative, and the renomination was rejected by a vote of 46 to 39.

Carrying out his threat, President Coolidge then tendered Warren a recess appointment. But the beleagured Michigan lawyer was weary of being at the center of a tug-of-war between two branches of the national government; he politely declined the president's offer.

Soon afterward Coolidge tried to fill the vacancy by sending to the Senate the nomination of John G. Sargent, a former attorney general of Vermont. Three hours later the Senate, having put the president in his place, confirmed the appointment.

The Newspaper That Would Not Stay Gagged

Chiseled in the marble of the facade of the *Chicago Tribune* building is a lengthy statement about freedom of the press that ends with this sentence: "The fact that liberty of the press may be abused by miscreant purveyors of scandal does not make any less necessary the immunity of the press from prior restraint in dealing with official misconduct."

This quotation is part of the opinion rendered by Chief Justice Charles Evans Hughes when the Supreme Court handed down its verdict in the celebrated case of *Near v. Minnesota*.

The First Amendment to the Constitution states that Congress shall make no law abridging the freedom of the press, and by the Fourteenth Amendment this prohibition was later extended to the states. For 140 years, ever since the Bill of Rights went into effect, it had been assumed that the Constitution forbade any form of government censorship of the press—prior restraint—such as had existed in England for a long time. Not until 1931 did the Supreme Court hear a case that questioned the principle of permitting newspapers to print the news as they saw it.

This case, *Near v. Minnesota*, came about as a result of an unusual 1925 Minnesota law that prohibited as a public nuisance the publication of newspapers and magazines that included material that was "malicious, scandalous and defamatory." In 1927 the county attorney of Hennepin

County had sought an injunction to halt future publication of the *Saturday Press*, a sleazy Minneapolis weekly that, in a series of articles, had charged that city and county officials were not arresting local Jewish gangsters who allegedly were operating gambling, bootlegging, and racketeering rings. The strongly anti-Semitic newspaper had claimed that the Minneapolis police chief was in collusion with the Jewish gangsters and that the county attorney had refused to take adequate measures to end the vice operations.

When this same county attorney had asked for a court order to stop publication of the newspaper, a sympathetic judge issued a temporary injunction shutting down the *Saturday Press* on the grounds that it was an anti-Semitic scandal sheet and thereby a public nuisance that had violated Minnesota's so-called Gag Law.

Jay M. Near, one of the publishers of the *Saturday Press*, refused to accept the court's verdict. While admitting that his paper had published defamatory stories, Near argued that forbidding its publication infringed on his rights under the First and Fourteenth Amendments. Jay appealed his case to the Minnesota Supreme Court, but it agreed with the ruling of the lower court.

Determined to have this decision reversed, Near then appealed to the highest court in the land. So the United States Supreme Court was faced with the task of deciding whether the Minnesota Gag Law was constitutional. At the heart of the Near case was this crucial question: Can a scandalous newspaper be permitted to continue its operation when some of its articles may be malicious, untrue, and subject to libel suits?

The justices were sharply divided; some of them strongly supported the Minnesota statute. Justice Pierce Butler declared that this statute did not "operate as a *previous* restraint on publication within the proper meaning of that phrase." The restraint, he contended, occurred only *after* publication of articles that were clearly a public nuisance, and it served only to prevent further illegal publications of the same kind. In Butler's opinion, nullifying the Minnesota Gag Law "exposes the peace and good order of every community" to "malicious assaults of any insolvent publisher who may have . . . sufficient capacity to contrive and put into effect a scheme or program for oppression, blackmail or extortion."

When Chief Justice Hughes called for the vote in this case, the count stood 4 to 4. It was left to him to cast the deciding vote. Hughes voted against the Minnesota statute; by the narrowest of margins, 5 to 4, prior restraint was ruled unconstitutional.

In rendering the majority opinion of the Court, Hughes asserted that the Minnesota Gag Law was "the essence of censorship." He said that suing for libel, not curtailing a newspaper, was the proper response to false charges and character assassination, and the chief justice emphasized that the freedom to criticize government officials was an important right of the American people.

Forty years after *Near v. Minnesota*, the Supreme Court had to decide an even more critical case involving government censorship of the press. In June 1971, the *New York Times* published the first of a series of articles based on a secret Defense Department account of America's controversial role in the Vietnam War. The classified information for these articles, which came to be called the Pentagon Papers, had been slipped to the *Times*, and later to the *Washington Post*, by Daniel Ellsberg, an antiwar protester and previous employee of the Defense Department and Rand Corporation. The Pentagon Papers revealed that major decisions about the Vietnam War had been made by government leaders in ways that intentionally deceived the American public.

The Justice Department asked for a temporary restraining order to prevent the *Times* from publishing the rest of the Pentagon Papers. Government lawyers contended that publishing these secret documents would greatly endanger national security and cripple the future conduct of American foreign affairs, which often require confidential dealings. The *Times* replied, on the other hand, that the American people were entitled to know the full facts about the war and the shameful deception of Washington officials.

After a federal judge granted the restraining order, the *Times* carried its case all the way to the Supreme Court. This enormously important case, which was on the front pages of newspapers throughout the country, required a speedy resolution, and the justices responded with unusual haste. On June 30, 1971 — only fifteen days after the government had first tried to censure the *Times* — the Court announced its decision. By a 6-3 vote, the Supreme Court declared that the *Times* could publish all of the Pentagon Papers. Following the precedent established by *Near v. Minnesota*, the Court once again firmly rebuked government censorship of the press.

A Stitch in Time Saves Nine

Franklin D. Roosevelt's New Deal triggered an earth-shaking economic revolution on a scale unrivaled in the history of the republic. In his first hundred days in the White House Roosevelt sent fifteen major bills to Congress, and all of them were passed. To many millions of Americans FDR was clearly the most popular president since his cousin Theodore, and in both houses of Congress he had a solid majority of Democrats eager to march to the beat of his drum.

There was one serious impediment, however, to the onward surge of the New Deal. Most of the federal judges were conservatives who had been appointed by Roosevelt's three Republican predecessors in the presidency; only 28 percent of the federal judiciary was Democratic. By the end of FDR's first thousand days in the White House, judges had issued some 1,600 injunctions pertaining to new federal laws, and over a thousand cases involving New Deal legislation were in litigation.

Some of these cases eventually would reach the Supreme Court, and the makeup of the nation's highest tribunal caused the president his greatest concern. Four of the justices—James C. McReynolds, George Sutherland, Willis Van Devanter, and Pierce Butler—were staunch conservatives. Nicknamed the "Four Horsemen," these four justices were consistently hostile to what liberals called "progressive" legislation. The liberal camp had only three justices, Louis D. Brandeis, Benjamin N. Cardozo, and Harlan F. Stone. Somewhere between the conservatives and the liberals stood Chief Justice Charles Evans Hughes and Justice Owen J. Roberts, but most of the time they voted with the Four Horsemen.

In January 1935, the process of judicial nullification began. On January 7, the Supreme Court struck down one section of the National Recovery Act, claiming that it illegally gave the president legislative authority to regulate the petroleum industry. A few months later the Court dealt a staggering blow to the New Deal. By a 5-4 vote it invalidated the Railroad Retirement Act on the grounds, first, that the government had deprived railroad companies without due process of law by forcing them to contribute to pensions for their employees; and, second, that Congress' control over interstate commerce was not so broad as to justify its interference in employer-employee relations. President Roosevelt knew that if the Court continued this line of reasoning, the all-important Social Security bill that was then before Congress would suffer the same fate.

The most crippling attacks on the New Deal were still to come. On

May 27, 1935, a day that liberals labeled "Black Monday," the Supreme Court declared that the NRA was unconstitutional for two reasons: it conferred legislative powers on the president, and the company involved in the case was not engaged in interstate commerce. On the same day the Court invalidated the Frazier-Lemke Act, designed to delay foreclosures of farm mortgages.

Early in 1936 the Supreme Court struck down the Agricultural Adjustment Act, which was the chief pillar of the New Deal program to help the nation's impoverished farmers. A few months later the Court nullified the Guffey-Snyder Coal Conservation Act, maintaining that the mining of coal was not interstate commerce. The highest court in the land had now denied that Congress had any jurisdiction over manufacturing, agriculture, and mining. Then, in June 1936, by a vote of 5 to 4, the Court ruled that the state of New York could not set a minimum wage for women.

By the summer of 1936 it was obvious that five or six willful men held in their hands the fate of nearly the entire New Deal and quite possibly the future of the nation for years to come. FDR angrily vented his frustration with the Court, declaring that the federal government could not deal successfully with any economic problems as long as the justices blindly clung to their "horse and buggy" definition of interstate commerce.

The 1936 presidential election returned Roosevelt to office by a landslide margin, and the congressional elections put the Democrats even more substantially in control of both houses. Buoyed by new confidence that the American people overwhelmingly supported his policies, FDR interpreted his massive election victory as a mandate to go to war against the handful of black-robed men who were obstructing the New Deal.

He hit upon the idea of increasing the number of Supreme Court justices (and other federal judges), so that he could add more New Deal partisans to the bench. It was not unprecedented to change the number of justices. The Supreme Court had begun with six justices in 1789, and its size was later changed five times before Congress, in 1869, set the number of justices at nine. The gist of FDR's plan was that when a Supreme Court justice did not retire within six months after reaching the age of seventy, a new judge could be added, up to a total of six. Since the average age of the justices then was seventy-eight, this act would have given the president the opportunity to pack the court with new members who were pro-New Deal.

When Roosevelt sent his judicial reorganization bill to Congress, it was heatedly debated both on and off Capitol Hill. Some of his ardent fans applauded FDR's bold plan to put an end to the Supreme Court's nullification of New Deal measures. But many people accused the president of seeking dictatorial powers by trying to "control the umpire." Even some of FDR's most loyal supporters in Congress strenuously objected to his tinkering with the checks-and-balances system that was the sancrosanct ideal upon which the national government had been founded. Congress turned down the plan, which was the first stinging defeat handed the president by a usually subservient legislature.

But while the court-packing debate raged in the halls of Congress and in living rooms across the country, an extraordinary sudden change occurred in the Supreme Court. Chief Justice Hughes and Justice Roberts started to side with the liberals on new cases that came before the Court. No one is certain why these justices changed their views, but it is possible that they adopted a more liberal stance in an effort to save the Court from the radical reorganization endorsed by the popular president.

On March 29, 1937, the Supreme Court in a 5-4 decision upheld the minimum wage law of the state of Washington. This was a complete about-face, since less than a year before the Court had nullified a similar New York minimum wage law for women under the due process clause. Now the Court was affirming that due process should not be used for the exploitation of labor and that the state had the right to regulate wages and hours. On that same day, March 29, the justices approved a new Frazier-Lemke Act protecting farmers with mortgages.

The supreme irony occurred on April 12, 1937, when the Supreme Court voted 5 to 4 to validate the National Labor Relations (Wagner) Act. This ruling involved a case in which the National Labor Relations Board had ordered the Jones and Laughlin Steel Corporation to reinstate ten employees dismissed for union activity. The circuit court had refused to enforce the order, claiming that it lay beyond the scope of federal power. But the Supreme Court, with its new liberal tilt, decided that industrial strife in the company did affect interstate commerce. Because the movement of goods was essential to the economy of the nation, the Court concluded that Congress had the power to prescribe labor relations at the factories in which the goods were manufactured. Thus, in this single sweeping stroke, collective bargaining became the law of the land.

Later, the Supreme Court approved the Social Security Act and a second Agricultural Adjustment Act, which was similar in many respects to the earlier AAA that the Court had overturned. So, while Roosevelt lost his battle to increase the size of the Court, he won the war to secure favorable judicial judgments on many of his New Deal measures. And it is entirely possible that his court-packing scheme was the spur that caused Justices Hughes and Roberts to suddenly view the New Deal agenda in a new light.

With the retirement and deaths of the elderly justices, the idea to enlarge the Supreme Court became academic. By 1941, Roosevelt had appointed the chief justice and seven of the eight associate justices of the Court. Ironically, FDR added more justices to the Supreme Court than any other president in history.

A Narrow Escape from National Peril

After 1938 no further New Deal legislation was passed by Congress. Most of the reform measures that FDR wanted already had been achieved, and there was a growing resistance in Congress to add to the list. Moreover, the president had to turn most of his attention to ominous events outside the United States.

Germany started World War II in September 1939 by invading Poland, a country that Hitler's awesome military machine conquered in a little less than a month. In the spring of 1940, Denmark, Norway, Holland, and Belgium fell like tenpins before the Nazi onslaught. German armies then drove deep into France and, on June 22, the proud French nation surrendered. Britain, soon to become the target of massive Nazi bombing, was the only outpost of freedom left in all western Europe.

When Hitler took the warpath, he was condemned in the United States as a cruel and selfish bully. But there was a widespread belief that Europe's quarrels were no business of the United States and that it was dangerous for us to meddle in them. All during the 1930s strong isolationist beliefs had completely dominated American foreign policy. And when the war clouds engulfed Europe, isolationists formed the America First Committee, which included powerful leaders in Congress, prominent newspaper publishers, and the famous aviator, Charles A. Lindbergh, who had inspected the German air force and concluded that it was unbeatable.

The first significant shift away from the isolationist position occurred after the fall of France and the imminent threat of a Nazi invasion of Britain. Public opinion polls showed that the proportion of Americans who believed a German victory would menace their security rose from 43 percent in March 1940 to 69 percent in July 1940, shortly after France had surrendered. The need to provide the United States with greater military strength became so apparent that Congress heeded FDR's warnings and between June and September 1940 appropriated a record 13 billion dollars for defense. Congress also voted to raise taxes, even though this was an election year.

At that time the United States armed forces were woefully weak. The Army had been legally limited to 375,000 men; it ranked seventeenth in total manpower and weapons among the armies of the world, without even the capacity of the late Polish army, which Hitler's forces had crushed in 27 days.

After the collapse of France, a proposal for conscription was introduced in the House by James W. Wadsworth, a Republican from New York, and in the Senate by Edward R. Burke of Nebraska, an anti–New Deal Democrat. But President Roosevelt, always the consummate politician, at first was reluctant to call for conscription. He was running for a third term in the White House, and FDR feared that the first peacetime draft in the nation's history could become a partisan issue that might drag him down to defeat. Still, public sentiment was steadily developing behind the draft bill. On June 25 the proportion of those who approved it in a public opinion survey was 59 percent; on July 20 this figure rose to 69 percent; in late August it stood at 86 percent. FDR continued to hesitate, but when his Republican opponent for the presidency, Wendell Willkie, endorsed the draft, the president also announced his support for the bill.

As Roosevelt had anticipated, isolationists adamantly opposed peacetime conscription. "If you pass the bill," shouted Montana Senator Burton K. Wheeler, "you accord Hitler his greatest and cheapest victory to date." Wheeler's Senate colleague from Montana, James Murray, protested: "A conscript army made up of youths trained for a year or two, compared to Hitler's army, is like a high school football team going up against the professional teams they have in Chicago and New York." Representative Martin L. Sweeney, an Irishman from Ohio, declared that the draft was nothing but a scheme to turn the United States over to British devils. Even labor leader John L. Lewis got into the act, thundering that conscription smacked of "dictatorship and fascism."

Yet, in spite of all the vociferous opposition, the Wadsworth-Burke bill sailed through Congress with comfortable margins in both houses. On October 16, 1940, over sixteen million men between eighteen and thirty-five registered for military service. About 900,000 of these men were to be drafted immediately for twelve months of training, after which they would pass into the reserves. According to the conscription law, no draftees were to be sent outside the Western Hemisphere.

In the months that followed, the United States became the "great arsenal of democracy." After the passage of the Lend-Lease Act in March 1941, huge supplies of war material were shipped to Britain and also to the Soviet Union after Hitler attacked that country in June. Without any doubt, the United States was drawing closer and closer to the life-and-death confrontation in Europe. On May 27, 1941, President Roosevelt proclaimed a state of national emergency, and, since the conscription law would expire in October, he asked Congress to extend the tenure of service for drafted men to 18 months. It was obvious, the president reminded Congress, that the defense effort would virtually collapse if the draftees were allowed to go home when their year's term expired.

FDR's political lieutenants warned him that the isolationists were determined to wage an all-out, large-scale war against extension of the draft. Senator Wheeler was sending out a million postcards urging citizens to write the president that they were opposed to American involvement in Europe's war. Other isolationists were alerting families of draftees across the country to promote a new national slogan — OHIO (Over the Hill in October) — which was a blunt invitation to draftees to desert if Congress lengthened their period of service.

The president, concerned by this growing avalanche of criticism, ordered highly respected Chief of Staff General George C. Marshall to address Congress and plea for the extension of the draft and the removal of the provision in the existing act that prohibited sending draftees outside the Western Hemisphere. On August 7, by a 45-30 vote, the Senate acceded to Marshall's request, but, even though war was near, there was tremendous pressure in the House to end the draft. Speaker Sam Rayburn begged his colleagues to put patriotism above the demands of outspoken constituents. "Do this for me," he implored. "I won't forget it." Rayburn personally coaxed and cajoled wavering congressmen, and a few of the laggards joined his cause.

The bill passed by one vote. On August 12, 1941, by a margin of 203 to 202, the House agreed to extend the draft. Less than four months later, the attack on Pearl Harbor plunged the United States into World War II.

Trying to Reduce the President's Powers

In November 1952, the Democrats' twenty-year hold on the White House came to an abrupt end with the election of Republican Dwight D. Eisenhower to the presidency. Voters also sent to Washington a Republican House and a Senate in which the GOP had a one-seat margin: forty-eight Republicans, forty-seven Democrats, and one Independent.

One change that many Republicans contemplated was the reduction of the powers of the president in the conduct of foreign affairs. They bristled with anger every time they recalled Franklin D. Roosevelt's agreement with Stalin at Yalta and charged that the Democratic president had betrayed China's interests at that meeting. And they expressed concern that other international agreements and treaties made by Presidents Roosevelt and Harry Truman portended a dangerous increase in the powers of the executive department.

The Republican-dominated Congress wasted no time in addressing this issue. A few days before Eisenhower took office, a constitutional amendment was proposed in the Senate that would have radically changed the process of making treaties and executive agreements. The senator who introduced this amendment was John W. Bricker, the former Ohio governor who had been the Republican vice presidential candidate in 1944. A dignified, handsome man with wavy white hair, Bricker was highly respected in conservative circles. His amendment had sixty-three cosponsors in the Senate and, on June 15, 1953, it was approved by the Judiciary Committee.

The major changes proposed by the Bricker amendment were: (1) to give Congress "power to regulate all Executive and other agreements with any foreign power or international organization"; and (2) to require that a "treaty should become effective as internal law in the United States only through legislation which would be valid in the absence of a treaty." This second provision, which was vaguely worded, led some constitutional experts to conclude that it meant each of the forty-eight states would have the authority to negate a treaty within its own jurisdiction.

There was strong sentiment throughout the country in favor of the Bricker amendment. Arrayed in support of the proposal were the American Legion, Daughters of the American Revolution, American Medical Association, Committee for Constitutional Government, *Chicago Tribune*, and the Vigilant Women for the Bricker Amendment — "a volunteer organization of housewives and mothers of boys overseas" — which brought to Capitol Hill petitions allegedly signed by over one-half million citizens.

The time seemed ripe for such an amendment. The American people were exasperated by the inconclusive drawn-out war against North Korea; Senator Joseph McCarthy was riding high in his crusade to uncover Communist subversives; there was a growing disenchantment with the United Nations, partly because it had been unable to keep the peace and partly because it was proposing many covenants that might contain provisions at variance with national or state laws. So Senator Bricker struck a responsive chord with large numbers of Americans when he warned against imposing on the United States "socialism by treaty," and when he insisted that his amendment sprang from a fear that "American sovereignty and the American Constitution . . . are threatened by treaty law."

Not all Americans, however, believed that the Bricker amendment should be added to the Constitution. Among those who opposed it were the League of Women Voters, the Americans for Democratic Action, both the *New York Times* and the *Washington Post*, and FDR's widow, Eleanor Roosevelt. But in time the biggest stumbling block to passage of the Bricker amendment would be the opposition of the Republican in the White House, President Eisenhower himself.

When he first learned of the amendment, at the time that he was preparing for his presidential inauguration, Eisenhower was sympathetic to its general purpose. He had criticized Presidents Roosevelt and Truman for extending the authority of the executive branch, and one of his campaign promises had been to try to restore the constitutional balance of power between the presidency and Congress. But before President Eisenhower commented publicly about the Bricker amendment, Secretary of State John Foster Dulles and other White House advisers had cautioned him to withhold judgment until the proposal had been carefully studied and thoroughly discussed by the officials of the new administration.

President Eisenhower asked his Cabinet and many prominent attorneys to give him their advice about this controversial amendment that one journalist said had launched "our greatest debate about the Constitutional ordering of our foreign relations since 1788." Dulles reported to the president that the Bricker amendment would curtail executive authority much too stringently and make it utterly impossible to conduct foreign affairs effectively. The secretary of state asserted that the amendment would "in large measure, reproduce the international impotence which marked the Confederation during the period preceding the adoption of our Constitution," when each state could conduct its own foreign affairs. If the amendment were adopted, Dulles warned, ". . . this would be taken by our friends and by our enemies as foreshadowing a revolutionary position in the United States."

Most of Eisenhower's advisers echoed Dulles's views, but the president was slow to commit himself. He wanted to find some middle ground that would avoid splitting the Republican party into two belligerent factions bound for "a head-on collision over this durn thing." So the president invited Senator Bricker to the White House to negotiate a compromise, but the amendment's chief sponsor would not budge on any of its major points. Finally, after three months of fruitless efforts to tone down the amendment, Eisenhower announced he opposed it, but even three months later he still was reluctant to urge any Republican to join him in opposition. Dulles chided the president about this at a Cabinet meeting in July 1953, saying, "We just have to make up our minds and stop being fuzzy about this."

"I haven't been fuzzy about this," the president snapped. "There was nothing fuzzy in what I told Bricker. I said we'd go just so far and no further."

"I know, sir," Dulles replied, "but you haven't told anybody else."

The 1953 session of Congress adjourned with no further action taken on the amendment, but it was back on the Senate agenda in January 1954. As the debate dragged on, the president's patience wore thin. On one occasion he raged, "I'm so sick of this I could scream! The whole damn thing is senseless and plain damaging to the prestige of the United States. We talk about the French not being able to govern themselves—and we sit here wrestling with the Bricker amendment." By early 1954 Eisenhower was painfully aware that the wrangling over this amendment was undermining his leadership of a nation that had assumed hegemony of the postwar free world. He resented innuendos in the press that he was only a "caretaker president" and the charge leveled by columnist Walter Lippmann that the country was witnessing an "abdication of the powers of the executive and the usurpation of Congress."

The president finally seized the initiative. In a strongly worded letter to Senate Majority Leader William Knowland on January 25, 1954, Eisenhower said:

> I am unalterably opposed to the Bricker amendment.... It would so restrict the conduct of foreign affairs that our country could not negotiate the agreements necessary for the handling of our business with the rest of the world. Such an amendment would make it impossible for us to deal effectively with friendly nations for our mutual defense and common interests.
>
> These matters are fundamental. We cannot hope to maintain

peace if we shackle the Federal Government so that it is no longer sovereign in foreign affairs. The President must not be deprived of his historic position as the spokesman for the nation in its relations with other countries.

Adoption of the Bricker amendment in its present form by the Senate would be notice to our friends as well as our enemies abroad that our country intends to withdraw from its leadership in world affairs. The inevitable reaction would be of major proportion. It would impair our hopes and plans for peace and for the successful achievement of the important international matters now under discussion. . . .

When this letter was released to the press, it bolstered the will of the senators who opposed the amendment and may have swung over some of the fence sitters. On February 25, 1953, the showdown came in the Senate. The Bricker amendment fell short of the two-thirds vote: 50 senators were for it and 42 against it.

The next day Senator Walter George of Georgia tried to extend an olive branch by offering a milder version of the Bricker amendment. It omitted the much-maligned provision that could have required that treaties must be approved by the states, but even so, the administration found the George amendment unacceptable because of restrictions placed on the president's powers to conduct foreign affairs. The Bricker stalwarts rallied their troops behind this new proposal and picked up the votes of some senators who had not supported the original amendment. Senator Knowland voted for it because, he later said, he could not ignore "a dangerous tendency toward executive encroachment on legislative powers." Some senators who were usually known as liberals also voted for the substitute amendment. These included Minority Leader Lyndon B. Johnson, Mike Mansfield, Margaret Chase Smith, and Clinton Anderson.

There were 60 yeas and 31 nays on the George amendment. That thirty-first nay saved President Eisenhower from a stinging political defeat. Had that vote been aye, the amendment would have had the two-thirds margin needed for a constitutional amendment. And if the George amendment had become the law of the land, the history of American foreign policy during the next three decades could have been vastly different.

The Rights of the Accused

Probably the most important and certainly, in time, the most controversial appointment by President Eisenhower occurred in 1953 when he named Earl Warren chief justice of the Supreme Court. Republican Warren previously had served as attorney general of California and later as the first three-term governor of that state. During his political career Warren had been regarded as a man whose moderate views were popular with the voters, so it was not unexpected that the Republicans selected him as their (unsuccessful) vice presidential candidate in 1948 or that Eisenhower nominated him to head the Supreme Court five years later.

Warren's reputation for moderation ended, however, nearly as soon as he took his seat on the high bench. The new chief justice argued that the Court must be guided by economic and social situations and not merely by legal precedents when handing down its decisions. The Warren Court, which prevailed for almost sixteen years, became the most liberal court in the nation's history and the most activist since John Marshall had served as chief justice in the early days of the republic. During Warren's tenure the Supreme Court rewrote, with enormous significance, important constitutional doctrines governing civil rights, church-state relations, the apportionment of voting districts, and the administration of criminal justice.

In perhaps its most famous decision, the Warren Court in 1954 declared racially segregated schools "inherently unequal" and, therefore, unconstitutional. In two other well-known decisions, the Court outlawed prayer and Bible reading in public schools. The Court voted unanimously in the school segregation case, and there was only one dissenting vote in the cases pertaining to school prayer and Bible reading.

The justices were almost evenly divided, however, in some of the most important cases dealing with the administration of criminal justice. In this area the need to protect the constitutional rights of persons accused of crimes clashed with society's needs: (1) to protect the rights of the victims of crimes; and (2) to enable law-enforcement officers to use effective means for apprehending and convicting criminals.

The first major 5-4 Warren Court decision regarding criminal justice was rendered in the case *Malloy* v. *Hogan* in 1964. William Malloy had been arrested during a gambling raid in Hartford, Connecticut. He was found guilty and given a suspended sentence. Later he was held in contempt by a state court for refusing to answer questions on the grounds of possible self-incrimination. The state court thus ruled that the Fifth Amendment was not applicable to state prosecutions.

When the *Malloy* case was appealed, the Supreme Court, by the narrow margin of one vote, overruled the decision of the Connecticut court. The highest court affirmed that, under the Fourteenth Amendment's due process clause, the Fifth Amendment protection against self-incrimination extended to state trials as well as federal trials.

The year before, the Supreme Court in *Gideon v. Wainwright* had declared, in a unanimous verdict, that the Sixth Amendment required that every person accused of a serious crime be provided the aid of an attorney. The Fifth Amendment safeguard against self-incrimination was linked with the Sixth Amendment right to counsel in the Supreme Court's rulings in the famous cases of *Escobedo v. Illinois* and *Miranda v. Arizona*.

One week after the *Malloy* decision, the Court announced its verdict in the case involving Danny Escobedo, who had been convicted of murder in Illinois. During his police interrogation, Escobedo repeatedly asked to consult with his attorney, but his request was denied. Incriminating statements he made at the time of his interrogation later were used as evidence against him at his trial. Escobedo challenged the conviction, claiming that because his right to counsel when the police questioned him had been violated, his trial had not been fair and the guilty verdict was an illegal action.

The Supreme Court voted 5 to 4 in favor of Escobedo. Justice Arthur J. Goldberg wrote the majority opinion and explained why the Court had reversed Escobedo's conviction. He declared that since the accused man had requested and been denied the opportunity to consult with his lawyer, and the police had not warned him of his constitutional right to remain silent, Escobedo had been "denied 'the Assistance of Counsel' in violation of the Sixth Amendment," and no statement elicited by police during the interrogation could be used against him in a criminal trial.

Justice Byron R. White, writing a dissenting opinion, sharply disagreed with the Court majority. He declared, " . . . the Court seems driven by the notion that it is uncivilized law enforcement to use an accused own's admission against him at his trial. . . . The right to counsel now not only entitles the accused to counsel's advice and aid in preparing for trial but stands as an impenetrable barrier to any interrogation once the accused has become a suspect."

About a year before the *Escobedo* case reached the Supreme Court, Ernesto Miranda was tried for kidnapping and rape in Arizona. Statements he had made during police interrogation were used as evidence against him, and he was convicted and imprisoned. Before they had interrogated him, however, the police had not advised him of his right to remain silent and his right to counsel. From prison, Miranda challenged his conviction, claiming that it had been illegally obtained because his constitutional rights had been violated.

By the same 5-4 vote as in the *Escobedo* case, the Supreme Court in 1966 upheld Miranda's challenge. Chief Justice Warren wrote the opinion for the majority. Warren asserted that there are " . . . constraints society must observe consistent with the federal Constitution in prosecuting individuals for crime." The chief justice stipulated how these constraints, or protective devices, must be used by the police to assure that the accused person's constitutional rights are not being denied. "Prior to any questioning, the person must be warned that he has a right to remain silent, that any statement he does make may be used as evidence against him, and that he has a right to the presence of an attorney, either retained or appointed."

The four members of the Court who disagreed with the *Miranda* verdict were concerned that it could permit many criminals to go unpunished for their crimes. "There is in my view," wrote Justice White, "every reason to believe that a good many criminal defendants, who otherwise would have been convicted on what this Court has previously thought to be the most satisfactory kind of evidence, will now under this new version of the Fifth Amendment, either not be tried at all or will be acquitted if the State's evidence, minus the confession, is put to the test of litigation."

The *Miranda* decision became a political issue that pitted fervent civil rights advocates against strong defenders of a justice system that would be tough on suspected criminals. When Richard M. Nixon ran for president in 1968, he vigorously assailed the Warren Court for its liberal, activist interpretation of the Constitution and its "pampering of criminals." If elected president, Nixon pledged that he would appoint justices to the Supreme Court who were conservatives that respected "law and order" more than the rights of perpetrators of crimes. Nixon kept his promise. In 1969, the newly elected president took advantage of Earl Warren's retirement to nominate the new chief justice, Warren E. Burger, a staunchly conservative appeals court judge. By 1971 Nixon had filled three more vacancies on the Supreme Court with men who, at the time of their appointments, were regarded as conservative supporters of "law and order."

While the Burger Court never reversed *Miranda*, it did permit some exceptions to the stringent rules that had been laid down for law enforcement officers. In a 5-4 decision in 1971, the Court decreed that even though statements made by a suspect before he was told of his rights could not be used as evidence against him, those statements could be used to question his credibility as a witness if he took the stand in his own defense and then contradicted what he had said before the trial began. In other cases the Burger Court ruled that authorities may use a statement by a defendant not warned of his rights to locate a prosecution witness, and that police need not stop to tell suspects their rights if a gun, knife, or bomb is present.

In June 1986, Burger retired from the Court, and President Ronald Reagan elevated Associate Justice William Rehnquist to the job of chief justice and named Appeals Judge Antonin Scalia to take Rehnquist's former seat. Both Rehnquist and Scalia have consistently held conservative views, and some legal experts have prediced that the Rehnquist Court may further weaken the restrictive provisions of the controversial *Miranda* decision.

A Second Constitutional Convention?

Another area in which the Warren Court played an activist, controversial role was the reapportionment of voting districts for state legislatures and the House of Representatives. The first major case in this area was *Baker v. Carr*, which the Court decided in 1962. This case involved voting districts in Tennessee that had not been changed since 1901, even though the state's constitution mandated reapportionment every ten years to conform to new population figures.

Between 1901 and 1960 urban counties in Tennessee had grown much larger, but the state's voting districts had remained the same. Consequently, Tennesseans who lived in cities and large towns charged that they were underrepresented in both houses of the state legislature. They claimed that only 40 percent of the state's population elected two-thirds of the members of the state's lower house, and less than 40 percent of the population elected two-thirds of the upper house.

The plaintiffs in this case, who were from urban areas, argued that their votes did not have as much power as the votes of rural residents in determining the makeup of the state legislature. So they sued on the grounds that they had been denied equal protection of the law under the Fourteenth Amendment.

100 / By a Single Vote!

When this case reached the Supreme Court, the constitutional question that the justices had to decide was whether the federal courts had jurisdiction over cases involving the reapportionment of state legislatures. The Court, by a 6-2 vote, answered this question in the affirmative, maintaining that it did have the authority to deal with the problem of unequal representation in state legislatures.

In subsequent decisions the Supreme Court adopted the principle "one person, one vote" as its yardstick for deciding reapportionment cases. Justice William O. Douglas defined this principle as "the idea that every voter is equal to every other voter in his state. . . ." The "one person, one vote" concept was applied in two separate 1964 cases in which the Court ordered that there must be voting districts of nearly equal size in the election of members of both houses of state legislatures and the House of Representatives.

A storm of angry protest erupted against the Court for meddling in the internal political affairs of the states. The most serious objection was unleashed at the Court decree that *both* houses of state legislatures must be based on population. At the national level one of the two legislative houses, the Senate, is based on geography rather than on population. So why should the states, argued the Court's critics, be denied the same right to use factors other than population in shaping the voting districts for one of their two houses?

Many voices in Congress were raised against the "one person, one vote" doctrine imposed by the Supreme Court. Heading the opposition forces on Capitol Hill was Everett M. Dirksen of Illinois, the Republican minority leader in the Senate. At the heart of Senator Dirksen's hostility toward the reapportionment rulings was a deep-seated fear that state legislatures would come under the complete control of urban areas, thereby depriving rural and small-town residents of the significant part they had traditionally played in decision making.

A flamboyant senator with an irrepressible flair for dramatic speeches, Dirksen was regarded by both friends and foes as a man with exceptional political skill and enormous clout. In late 1964 he nearly pushed through the Senate an injunction that would have delayed the Court's reapportionment directives, but Democrats and Republicans from large urban areas banded together to defeat his proposal. Dirksen had lost round one of his battle, but the war was far from over. The wily senator reckoned that there was one sure way to negate a controversial judicial decision—by a constitutional amendment.

On January 6, 1965, Dirksen introduced in the Senate the following amendment to the U.S. Constitution: "The people of a state may apportion one house of a bicameral legislature using population, geography, or political subdivisions as factors, giving each factor such weight as they deem appropriate." In arguing for his proposed amendment, Dirksen declared that neither the Constitution nor congressional legislation gave the Supreme Court any legal right to interfere with the makeup of state legislatures. The Illinois senator convinced many of his colleagues that his argument was sound and his cause was just. When the roll was called in the Senate, the tally was 57 to 39 in favor of the Dirksen amendment, but this was seven votes short of the necessary two-thirds margin. The following year Dirksen presented the amendment again, and the Senate approved it a second time, but again by less than a two-thirds vote.

Still, Dirksen would not give up the fight. "Unlike old soldiers," he said, paraphrasing General Douglas MacArthur's famous statement, "a basic issue neither dies nor fades away." The determined senator knew that the Constitution provides a way to propose a constitutional amendment without getting the approval of both houses of Congress. If two-thirds of the state legislatures petition Congress to call a constitutional convention to propose an amendment, then Congress must honor this request. Deciding to try this seldom-used approach to promote his amendment, Dirksen carried his crusade to state legislatures throughout the country.

Thirty-four states had to petition Congress before the constitutional convention would be summoned. By the end of 1966, twenty-eight states had jumped on the Dirksen bandwagon. Four more states were added in the next two years. Iowa joined the group on 1969. Thirty-three states had now petitioned Congress to call a constitutional convention, just one state short of the needed number.

Then, for various reasons, the campaign to have a new constitutional convention began to lose momentum. Opponents of Dirksen started challenging the validity of many of the petitions from the state legislatures. Democratic Senator William Proxmire of Wisconsin alleged that all but six of the petitions were "illegally constituted." Constitutional experts pointed out that not all of the petitions agreed in wording or even in purpose.

Moreover, some supporters of the Dirksen proposal began to have second thoughts about holding another constitutional convention. They grew concerned about the jurisdiction of such a convention. Would it restrict itself to the one question of reapportionment? Or would it go far astray and try to change parts of the Constitution, perhaps even tampering with the Bill of Rights and the Fourteenth Amendment? No one knew the answers to these questions because neither the Constitution nor congressional legislation ever laid down any guidelines pertaining to a constitutional convention.

Pressure was brought to bear on many state lawmakers to switch their votes, and in six states one house of the legislature did pass a resolution that repealed its earlier measure favoring the convention. And when Senator Dirksen died in September 1969, the strongest voice for the convention was silenced. As time passed, in state after state the voting districts gradually were reshaped as the Supreme Court had demanded.

It is interesting to speculate what might have happened if just one more state had petitioned Congress to hold a new constitutional convention. Would this have spurred both houses of Congress to accept the Dirksen amendment rather than call the convention? Would legal challenges to the state petitions have put the entire matter back into the courts? If the convention had proceeded, would it have acted only on the "one person, one vote" issue and then adjourned? And would there have been modern counterparts to James Madison, George Washington, and Benjamin Franklin, with enough wisdom and foresight to steer the convention around dangerous pitfalls to a successful conclusion?

Lowering the Voting Age

The notion that youths reach adulthood at the age of twenty-one is rooted deeply in history. In England during the Middle Ages the armor that knights wore was very heavy, and a young man was not considered physically strong enough to bear it until he was twenty-one. So the tradition developed that twenty-one was the age when a squire could become a knight and a youth could become an adult.

When the English colonists in the New World drew up their first charters, twenty-one became the minimum age for voting. This age requirement later was written into state constitutions and persisted in nearly all the states until 1971. Through all these years many older people believed that youths were "too poorly informed" or "too radical" or "not mature enough" to be entrusted with the precious ballot. Also, it was said that if young people were not yet making their own living but could go to the polls, they might vote to spend taxes derived from "somebody else's hard-earned income." The opposition against lowering the voting age was formidable; by 1954, thirty-seven states had considered this possibility, but, with the exception of Georgia, all of them had voted against it.

Only when the United States was at war did a substantial proportion of adults favor the eighteen-year-old vote. In 1939, shortly before the beginning of World War II, a Gallup poll revealed that 79 percent of the American people were against lowering the voting age. But in 1942, after the United States had been drawn into the war, the cry of "old enough to fight, old enough to vote" pricked many consciences, and only 42 percent of the people polled said they opposed the younger voting age. In that same year Congressman Jennings Randolph, a West Virginia Democrat, introduced in the House of Representatives a constitutional amendment calling for the eighteen-year-old vote. The most opposition to this amendment came from southern Democrats who feared that it would interfere with the rights of states to impose their own voting qualifications and thus obstruct their long-established methods of preventing blacks from voting. The Southerners squashed Randolph's amendment, and after the war the public's interest in this subject waned.

Persistent members of both houses of Congress tried many times to reduce the voting age. Between 1952 and 1970 more than 150 versions of Randolph's amendment were circulated in the corridors of Capitol Hill— all to no avail.

During and immediately after the Korean War, there was renewed interest in letting youth vote, this time with the full backing of the man in the White House. "For years our citizens between the ages of eighteen and twenty-one have, in times of peril, been summoned to fight for America," declared President Dwight D. Eisenhower in his State of the Union message in January 1954. "They should participate in the political process that produces this fateful summons. I urge Congress to propose to the states a constitutional amendment permitting citizens to vote when they reach the age of eighteen."

This prodding by the president helped push an amendment for lowering the voting age through the Senate Judiciary Committee and onto the floor for debate. There Senator Richard Russell of Georgia led the fight against the amendment, declaring that, according to the Constitution, only the states had the right to set voting qualifications. When the senators voted on this measure, 34 were in favor of the amendment and 24 against, so it fell five votes short of the two-thirds needed to amend the Constitution. Another sixteen years would pass before the Senate voted again on the eighteen-year-old vote.

Meanwhile, several states had considered lowering the voting age but only four took affirmative action. Georgia had given the vote to eighteen-year-olds in 1943, Kentucky in 1955. When the new states of Hawaii and Alaska had entered the Union in 1959, their state constitutions extended the vote to youth, at age twenty in Hawaii and nineteen in Alaska. The other forty-six states rigidly adhered to the longstanding tradition that a person under twenty-one could not vote.

The Vietnam War was the catalyst that turned this situation around. Thousands of young draftees were risking their lives on Asian battlefields in a war that many Americans neither understood nor accepted. Thousands of other youth were fervent political activists. They protested against the war; they worked for racial desegregation and equality of the sexes; they campaigned for a cleaner environment. Young Americans demanded the right to be heard and the right to express their feelings at the polls.

At last, the legislators on Capitol Hill were listening sympathetically to the young people's pleas. "Can we, in good conscience, expect youth to work within the system when we deny them that very opportunity?" asked Senator Birch Bayh of Indiana.

Another senator, Edward Kennedy of Massachusetts, declared that providing eighteen-year-olds with the vote was "the most important single principle we can pursue as a nation if we are to succeed in bringing our youth into full and lasting participation in our institutions of democratic government."

Conservative Senator Barry Goldwater of Arizona, who had been the Republican presidential candidate in 1964, said bluntly, ". . . I think we have studied this issue long enough. The voting age should be lowered and lowered at once across the entire nation."

Because of the difficulty in getting a constitutional amendment approved, Senator Mike Mansfield of Montana, another supporter of lowering the voting age, tried a different strategy. He added a provision giving eighteen-year-olds the vote to a bill that was then being debated in the Senate. This bill, which extended for another five years a law that protected the voting rights of blacks, needed only a majority vote of both houses to pass. The Senate and House of Representatives passed the bill and sent it to President Richard Nixon for his signature.

At first President Nixon hesitated to sign the bill into law. He said that he favored lowering the voting age but feared that the bill Congress had approved might be declared unconstitutional because it interfered with the states' rights to determine voting qualifications. Nevertheless, after deliberating a few days, the president signed the bill, which was then called the Voting Rights Act of 1970. President Nixon explained his support for this act in these words: "The reason the voting age should be lowered is not that eighteen-year-olds are old enough to fight. It is because they are smart enough to vote. Youth today is not as young as it used to be."

As Nixon and others had anticipated, the act was immediately challenged in the courts. The day after the president signed it, five New York voters asked a federal district court to declare it unconstitutional. They claimed that the new law (which not only lowered the voting age, but also ended residency requirements and suspended literacy tests for voters) reduced the relative weight of their votes because it permitted millions of additional citizens to add their names to the voting lists. A short time later, the states of Oregon and Texas asked the Supreme Court to negate the law. Oregon had recently held a referendum on lowering the voting age, and the voters had rejected this ballot measure. Texas insisted that Congress, by changing the voting requirements, denied the states powers granted to them alone under the Constitution.

The Supreme Court was divided on this crucial issue. Four justices believed the younger voting age was constitutional for both federal and state elections, and four other justices felt that it was unconstitutional for any elections. The deciding vote had to be cast by elderly Justice Hugo Black, a Southerner who had been appointed to the Court by President Franklin D. Roosevelt in 1937.

Justice Black did not completely agree with either side. He believed that Congress had "ultimate supervisory power" over federal elections (elections for president, vice president, and members of Congress), but not over state and local elections. "It is a plain fact of history," he wrote, "that the Framers [of the Constitution] never imagined that the national Congress would set the qualifications for voters in every election from President to local constable or village alderman."

Since Justice Black's single vote would determine the constitutionality of the Voting Rights Act of 1970, the Supreme Court had to accept his point of view. By a 5-4 vote it ruled that the act was valid for federal elections but did not apply to state elections.

This unusual Court decision threatened to disrupt the states' election procedures. All of the states (except Georgia and Kentucky, which allowed eighteen-year-olds to vote) would have had to establish two separate systems of registration and voting, one for federal elections and the other for state and local elections. This could have caused vast confusion for election officials and the expenditure of millions of dollars to set up and maintain two different systems for elections.

The serious drawbacks of dual election systems prompted many groups and individuals to support a constitutional amendment that would make eighteen the minimum age for voting in all elections. Common Cause and the League of Women Voters were two of the national organizations that lobbied for this amendment. Youth groups, college political clubs, church councils, and prominent members of both political parties worked hard to convince legislators that the time now was ripe for proposing again a constitutional amendment to lower the voting age.

Congress responded by putting the amendment at the top of its agenda for the 1971 session. With a groundswell of public opinion solidly behind the measure, both houses swiftly approved it. Thirty-eight states still had to ratify the amendment before it could become part of the Constitution. Political experts, mindful of the states' rights argument that had been a stumbling block for such a long time, predicted that the ratification process would take at least a year. But states that had previously turned down the lower voting age now accepted it in preference to holding two separate elections, and the amendment sped through the ratification process in the record time of a little more than three months.

On June 30, 1971, the Twenty-sixth Amendment was added to the Constitution. It stated briefly but clearly that "the right of citizens of the United States, who are eighteen years of age or older, to vote shall not be denied or abridged by the United States or by any state on account of age." This amendment immediately gave the ballot to more than 11 million young Americans who, for the first time, had the opportunity to participate fully in the process that makes democracy work.

The Court Zigzags on Capital Punishment

The Eighth Amendment forbids "cruel and unusual" punishment, but it does not specify which kinds of punishment fit this definition. The framers of the Bill of Rights undoubtedly intended to outlaw barbaric forms of punishment that were practiced in the eighteenth century, such as branding, drawing and quartering, mutilating, and tar and feathering. But was the death penalty itself — if administered in a humane way — cruel and unusual punishment? The Bill of Rights does not say, and the Supreme Court has frequently reversed its position on this controversial issue.

The Court decided its first capital punishment case in 1879 when it decreed that a convicted murderer could be sentenced to death by a firing squad. Many years passed before the Court made other major rulings about the death penalty. In 1947 the justices were faced with a bizarre case in which a convicted murderer had been sentenced to death, but the electric chair had not worked properly and the man's life was spared. By a 5-4 vote, the Supreme Court declared that it was constitutional to subject this convict to a "second electrocution." In *McGautha* v. *California* in 1971, the Court, by a vote of 6 to 3, upheld a state law that left completely to the discretion of the jury the decision to impose the death penalty on a convicted defendant.

The next year, however, the Supreme Court did an about-face and reversed its *McGautha* ruling. The Court handed down decisions in three related cases: *Furman* v. *Georgia, Branch* v. *Texas*, and *Jackson* v. *Georgia*. By a vote of 5 to 4 in all three cases, the Court invalidated existing death penalty laws on the grounds that they violated the Eighth and Fourteenth Amendments. The five justices in the majority had been members of the activist Warren Court: William Brennan, Thurgood Marshall, William O. Douglas, Byron White, and Potter Stewart. The four dissenters were the Nixon appointees: Chief Justice Warren Burger, Harry Blackmun, Lewis F. Powell, Jr., and William Rehnquist.

Nine separate opinions were written on this controversial ruling. Two of the justices in the majority, Brennan and Marshall, felt that standards of decency had evolved to the point where capital punishment no longer could be tolerated under any circumstances. Justice Brennan wrote that the death penalty was "uniquely degrading to human dignity" and that there was no reason to think that it "serves any penal purpose more effectively than the less severe punishment of imprisonment."

The three other justices in the majority were unwilling to go as far in opposing the death penalty as Justices Brennan and Marshall did. They focused on the procedures by which some convicts were selected for the death penalty rather than on the actual punishment inflicted. As Justice Stewart pointed out, only a few convicted defendants were executed while many others were sent to prison for the same crimes. He declared that death sentences which were left to the discretion of juries were "wantonly" and "freakishly" imposed.

These 1972 decisions effectively put an end to death penalty laws in all the states. The Court, however, seemed to leave open two avenues states could follow in rewriting their capital punishment laws. One was to make the death penalty mandatory for specific crimes. This would eliminate the "wanton" and "freakish" aspects of laws that let some criminals be executed while others lived. The second avenue was to provide a two-stage procedure in trials involving crimes punishable by death. In the first stage, the guilt or innocence of the defendant would be decided. In the second stage, a separate hearing would be held for convicted defendants to determine whether the circumstances justified a sentence of death.

Thirty-five states passed new death penalty laws. Ten states followed the first avenue; they made the death penalty mandatory for certain crimes, such as killing a police officer or murder done while committing rape, arson, or kidnap. The other twenty-five states chose the two-step procedure.

Four years later, in 1976, the two types of state laws came before the Supreme Court. On the question of the mandatory death sentence the Court zigzagged again. The Court struck down, in 5-4 decisions, mandatory laws in North Carolina and Louisiana that had made death the required punishment for all defendants convicted of first-degree murder. The Court majority concluded that mandatory death laws "simply papered over the problems of unguided and unchecked jury discretion" and were unconstitutional because they showed no consideration for the individual defendant or for any special circumstances pertaining to the crime.

It appeared that the Supreme Court was on the verge of declaring the death penalty itself unconstitutional. But on the same day that the Court overturned the mandatory death penalty laws in North Carolina and Louisiana, it upheld, by a vote of 7 to 2, the two-stage procedures that were followed in three other states. In one of these cases, *Gregg* v. *Georgia*, seven members of the Court agreed that "the punishment of death does not invariably violate the Constitution." Writing for the majority, Justice Stewart said that the death penalty "is an extreme sanction, suitable to the most extreme of crimes."

Since the Court's 1976 rulings, it has been more consistent in cases involving capital punishment. It has upheld as constitutional the two-stage procedure adopted by twenty-five states, and it has generally struck down state laws making the death penalty mandatory for certain crimes. In 1977, the Court declared unconstitutional a Georgia law that made rape a crime punishable by death and a Louisiana law that made the death penalty mandatory for a person convicted of the first-degree murder of a police officer. And in 1978 the highest court in the land struck down Ohio's death penalty law for murder because it did not allow for mitigating factors that should be considered before the sentence of death was imposed.

What Is Obscenity?

One of the most vexing problems in American society is what to do about obscenity and pornography. On the one hand, there are charges that a magazine, book, or film is vulgar, lewd, filled with smut. On the other hand, there are claims that this same material must not be banned because it has literary, creative, or artistic values. Conflicts occur frequently between the individual's right of free expression and society's responsibility to protect the morals and welfare of the community. Invariably, many of these conflicts have found their way into the courts, and many obscenity cases have been appealed to the Supreme Court.

The authors of the Bill of Rights said nothing about protecting obscenity in the First Amendment. The Court has always ruled that obscene materials that have no redeeming social value and are distributed to appeal entirely to one's sexual interest can be quashed by national and state laws. But, as the Court came to find, it is very difficult to define precisely just what obscenity is. In one eleven-year period, 1957 to 1968, the Court decided thirteen cases involving the definition of obscenity and the justices rendered fifty-five separate opinions. Some justices, mindful of the elasticity of the First Amendment, defined obscenity in lenient terms; others, believing that vulgar materials deserved no protection, applied strict standards. Still others agreed with Justice Potter Stewart when he said he opposed "hard-core" obscenity but conceded that the only definition he could offer was "I know it when I see it."

Justice William Brennan summed up the Court's frustration with this troublesome issue when he said in 1973, "No other aspect of the First Amendment has, in recent years, demanded so substantial a commitment of [the Court's] time, generated such a disharmony of views, and remained so resistant to the formulation of stable and manageable standards as obscenity."

The Court first ventured to define obscenity when it heard the case of *Roth* v. *United States* in 1957. Samuel Roth had been convicted in New York of violating the federal obscenity law by mailing obscene books, circulars, and advertising material. By a 6-3 vote, the Court ruled that the law Roth broke was constitutional. Writing for the majority, Justice Brennan declared:

> ... All ideas having even the slightest redeeming social importance — unorthodox ideas, controversial ideas, even ideas hateful to the prevailing climate of opinion — have the full protection of the guaranties, unless excludable because they encroach upon the limited areas

of more important interests. But implied in the history of the First Amendment is the rejection of obscenity as utterly without redeeming social importance.

Justice Brennan then proposed this standard for defining obscenity. A work is guilty of obscenity if, to the "average person, applying community standards, the dominant theme of the material taken as a whole appeals to the prurient interest."

In 1966, the Supreme Court heard the obscenity case of *Ginzburg* v. *United States*. Ralph Ginzburg had used the mail to advertise three publications. The charge against him was not that the publications were obscene, but rather that the advertising of these materials through the mail openly appealed to the erotic interest of potential customers. By a 5-4 vote, the Court ruled against Ginzburg. Justice Brennan, writing the opinion of the majority, explained that the publications were advertised in such a way that they accentuated sexual feelings. On the other hand, the four dissenters branded the decision as a violation of the First Amendment and denounced the principle that nonobscene materials could be considered pornographic merely because of the advertising.

Then in 1973 the Supreme Court again wrestled with the definition of obscenity, and again the justices sharply disagreed. In *Miller* v. *California* the defendant had sent sexually explicit materials through the mail. These were brochures advertising four books and a movie that showed men and women performing sexual acts. California attempted to apply its criminal obscenity law to prosecute the defendant. The case revolved, in part, on the issue of whether the questionable materials should be judged by national standards or by standards established by a state.

Five justices voted to uphold the California law; four justices voted to invalidate it. By the slim margin of a single vote, the Supreme Court set up a standard, still in effect today, that gave governments at all levels much more latitude to prohibit obscene materials than did earlier Court rulings. States and local communities may regulate works that depict or describe sexual conduct, the Court decreed, providing they follow three basic guidelines. These are: (1) whether the average person, applying contemporary standards, would find the work as a whole appealing to the prurient interest; (2) whether the work depicts in a patently offensive way sexual conduct specifically defined by the applicable state or community law; and (3) whether the work as a whole lacks serious artistic, literary, political, or scientific value. Under this rule, the Court effectively declared that local standards rather than a national definition of obscenity may be used.

Chief Justice Warren Burger expressed the opinion of the majority when he wrote, "To equate the free and robust exchange of ideas and political debate with commercial exploitation of obscene material demeans the grand conception of the First Amendment and its high purposes in the historic struggle for freedom."

The four dissenters were not convinced that Chief Justice Burger's reasoning was correct. Justice William O. Douglas angrily claimed that "Since 'obscenity' is not mentioned in the Constitution or Bill of Rights," it cannot constitutionally be punished.

The Court's definition of obscenity in the *Miller* case probably raised as many questions as it answered. What was meant by the phrase that a questionable work must have serious value, Justice Brennan wondered? Until this case, he explained, "the protections of the First Amendment have never been thought limited to expressions of *serious* literary or political value." Who are the "average" people that decide what the "contemporary community standards" are? Must their attitudes pass some type of litmus test to determine if they are orthodox and conventional? Is a community a town, a county, or, in the eyes of the courts, an entire state?

Chief Justice Burger claimed that there is no reason why "the people of Maine and Mississippi" should "accept public depiction of conduct found tolerable in Las Vegas or New York City. . . . People in different states vary in their tastes and attitudes, and this diversity is not to be strangled by the absolutism of imposed uniformity."

Undoubtedly, attitudes do vary in different parts of the United States, but this only prompts more questions by critics of the *Miller* decision. Should the protections of the First Amendment change when a person crosses county lines or state borders? Is it logical and just that a person can buy a certain book or see a certain movie in Los Angeles but not in Atlanta? The knotty question—what is obscenity—still evades a definitive answer, and, quite likely, it always will.

Affirmative Action and Reverse Discrimination

In the 1960s Congress passed several acts to help eradicate discrimination against minorities. One of these acts, the Civil Rights Act of 1964, forbade employers to discriminate against a person on the basis of race, color, religion, sex, or national origin in any program receiving federal financial assistance. But even with this new Civil Rights Act, blacks and other minorities still lagged far behind whites in many ways. They had a much lower average income, less education, poorer housing and health facilities, and fewer people in the professions, such as law and medicine. For example, only about 2 percent of the nation's doctors were black, yet blacks constituted more than 10 percent of the total population.

In an effort to reduce inequities in employment and education, President Lyndon B. Johnson in 1965 issued executive orders calling for businesses to create more jobs and universities more educational opportunities for minorities and women. Described as "affirmative action," these orders were intended to raise the status of groups that were handicapped by existing discrimination and the effects of past discrimination. Consequently, many employers and educational institutions began opening more doors to the disadvantaged.

University and college admissions offices started giving special preferential treatment to minority groups. In time, however, this led to a new problem. Were the rights of qualified white persons violated when they were denied entrance to a university because a number of positions at the school were reserved for minority students who, in some cases, might be less qualified? If so, were the white persons the victims of "reverse discrimination"?

The Supreme Court first dealt with this problem in the 1974 case of *DeFunis* v. *Odegaard*. Marco DeFunis, Jr., had applied twice for admission to the University of Washington law school, and both times he had been turned down. Since the qualifying test scores included in his second application and his undergraduate grades were higher than those of a number of minority applicants who were accepted, DeFunis felt he had been unfairly denied admission and took his case to court. The judge ruled in his favor and ordered the university to admit him. But while DeFunis was a student at the law school, the lower court ruling was reversed by the Washington Supreme Court, which said that the school's admissions policy did not have a stigmatizing effect on nonminorities.

Knowing that he could be expelled at any time, DeFunis took his case to the Supreme Court.

By the time that the Supreme Court decided his case, DeFunis was about to graduate. So the Court, by a 5-4 vote, took the easy way out of this predicament. Five justices agreed that the case was moot (no longer a controversy) because their decision would have no effect on DeFunis, who was within a few months of graduation. The four dissenting justices were displeased because their colleagues had ducked an issue that almost certainly would surface again.

Four years later the question of reverse discrimination did return to the Supreme Court in a case that was widely publicized by the media. Allan Bakke, a white engineer, twice had been denied admission to the medical school of the University of California at Davis. To ensure minority representation in its student body, the Davis medical school, which took one hundred new students each year, set aside sixteen openings for "economically and educationally disadvantaged minority students." In each year that Bakke's application had been rejected, the school did accept some minority students with qualifications inferior to his. So Bakke brought suit, charging that the Davis "quota system" for minorities violated the California Constitution, the equal protection clause of the Fourteenth Amendment, and Title VI of the Civil Rights Act of 1964.

A superior court judge ruled that the Davis admissions policy had discriminated against Bakke because of race and, therefore, was invalid. When the school appealed the case to the California Supreme Court, it ruled unanimously that Davis's application of affirmative action was unconstitutional because it deprived whites of the equal protection of their rights. The medical school was ordered to admit Bakke.

This could have ended the matter, but the Davis officials appealed the case to the U.S. Supreme Court. When *University of California Regents v. Bakke* was laid before the highest court, the justices recognized that they had two fundamental questions to answer: (1) Had Bakke been the victim of reverse discrimination because of Davis's quota system; and (2) were all affirmative action programs unconstitutional?

Four members of the Court—Chief Justice Warren Burger and Justices William Rehnquist, Potter Stewart, and John Paul Stevens—agreed that Bakke's rights had been violated under Title VI of the 1964 Civil Rights Act and that it was unnecessary to decide whether they also had been violated under the Constitution. In the words of Justice Stevens, the Civil Rights Act "required a colorblind standard on the part of the government. . . . Under Title VI it is not permissible to say 'yes' to one person, but to say 'no' to another person, only because of the color of his skin." Four other justices—William Brennan, Thurgood Marshall, Harry Blackmun, and Byron White—voted to uphold the medical school's admissions policy including its quota system as a legitimate, appropriate means for helping to provide equal opportunities for minorities.

Justice Lewis F. Powell, Jr., held the deciding vote in this clash of opinions between the two groups of justices. Justice Powell cast his vote in favor of Bakke, but for a different reason than that expressed by the four other justices who sided with Bakke. He contended that the Davis medical school had erred because its admissions policy denied equal protection of the laws and thus was unconstitutional. With Powell providing the fifth and crucial vote, the Supreme Court declared that rigid quotas such as those used at Davis were illegal.

The important question of the legality of affirmative action programs still was unanswered. On this issue the Court again was sharply divided. Justices Brennan, Marshall, Blackmun, and White approved the use of affirmative action programs to reduce discrimination. In opposition, four of the other five justices who had supported Bakke claimed that the question of whether race could be considered a factor in college admissions did not have to be settled in the case they were hearing.

Justice Powell again was the man in the middle; his vote would swing the decision either way. He voted to uphold affirmative action, arguing that while inflexible numerical quotas based on race alone were unconstitutional, universities did have the right to develop a student body consisting of racially diverse individuals. Race, he felt, could be treated as a "plus" in admissions decisions when it was considered along with other factors. But Justice Powell cautioned that affirmative action programs should be limited to situations in which discrimination had been proved.

So, due mainly to the ambivalence of tie-breaking Justice Powell, both sides could claim at least a partial victory in *University of California Regents* v. *Bakke*. Critics of the Davis admissions policy were pleased that Bakke was admitted to the medical school and that rigid quotas were abolished. On the other hand, civil rights groups were pleased that affirmative action programs had been given the approval of the high court.

In September 1978, six years after he had first applied to medical school, Allan Bakke's persistence finally was rewarded; he became a first-year medical student at Davis. Four years later, at age 42, he graduated and was given a standing ovation by his classmates. Bakke then returned to his home state of Minnesota and became an anesthesiologist at the Mayo Clinic.

A Judicial Appointment in Jeopardy

In the first five-and-one-half years of his administration, President Ronald Reagan named 267 of the 752 judges on the federal bench — judges of the district courts, circuit courts of appeal, and the Supreme Court. Most of these judges shared the president's political philosophy, and their lifetime appointments offered Reagan his best hope of leaving a lasting conservative imprint on American society after he left office.

The Republican-dominated Senate usually confirmed the president's choices for the bench without heated controversy or prolonged debate. Such was not the case, however, in 1986 when Reagan named Daniel A. Manion, a lawyer from South Bend, Indiana, to fill a vacancy on the U.S. Seventh Circuit Court of Appeals. Many law school deans, the 1,400-member Chicago Council of Lawyers, and liberal politicians vehemently protested Manion's appointment to the second-highest level of courts in the nation. They charged that Manion's legal record was mediocre at best, and criticized some of his legal briefs for being poorly written and laced with spelling and grammatical errors. His critics also repeatedly referred to the fact that Manion, who had little experience practicing law outside state courts, had been given the lowest acceptable rating by the American Bar Association.

Manion's appointment had to be confirmed by the Senate, and Democratic senators did not confine their campaign against him to his record as an attorney. They also challenged his ideological views. Manion's conservative ideas had become widely known in Indiana during the 1970s, when he often appeared on radio and television programs with his father, Clarence Manion, a founder of the right-wing John Birch Society. Manion's opponents contended that his conservatism could affect his willingness to conform his own judicial opinions with those of the Supreme Court. They pointed out, for example, that as an Indiana state senator, Manion had sponsored a 1981 bill permitting the posting of the Bible's Ten Commandments in public schools only two months after the Supreme Court had overturned a similar Kentucky law. Manion's critics also cited his strong endorsement in 1977 of a book by the late archconservative Representative Larry P. McDonald that said "a Supreme Court decision is not the law of the land" and that labeled as unconstitutional both the Supreme Court's 1954 school desegregation decision and the 1964 Civil Rights Act.

Testifying at his confirmation hearing, Manion distanced himself from his earlier stands and promised to follow the rulings laid down by the Supreme Court. Many lawyers and some judges in Indiana and Illinois, including several of his political foes, came to Manion's defense, praising him as a competent attorney and a reasonable man.

Republican Robert Dole of Kansas, the Senate majority leader, angrily charged that Manion had become the unfortunate pawn in a political battle between liberals and conservatives. ". . . I think the stakes are not Mr. Manion," Dole declared. "The stakes are who's going to control the Senate, and can the Democrats get any political mileage out of torpedoing some young man from Indiana because he's a small-town lawyer, even though he has a qualified recommendation from the American Bar Association."

Echoing Dole's opinion, Senator Orrin G. Hatch of Utah said, "This is an ideological attack. There's no question about it." An ardent supporter of Manion, Hatch asserted that the president "has the right to appoint judges who share his political philosophy."

Democratic Senator Alan Cranston of California did not agree with Hatch. He argued that it was important for senators to weigh a nominee's philosophy—in addition to his qualifications—in deciding how to vote on his confirmation. Cranston maintained that an ideological extremist on either side of the political spectrum, "can create a doctrinal conflict of interest fully as inappropriate as a financial conflict of interest." Senators may need to know a nominee's views, Cranston believed, ". . . to determine whether they are within a range of reasonableness, whether the nominee is willing to follow controlling law and seems fair-minded and sufficiently sensitive to the temper of the times."

The question of Manion's confirmation promised to provide a very close contest. When the vote was taken, the result was a 47-47 tie. Then Senate Minority Leader Robert C. Byrd, a Democrat from West Virginia, switched his vote to the affirmative side in a parliamentary maneuver that allowed him to ask for reconsideration.

When the Senate balloted to decide whether to reconsider Manion's nomination on July 23, 1986, the vote again was tied, this time 49 to 49. A tie vote was sufficient to kill the motion to reconsider the appointment, but Vice President George Bush added his tie-breaking vote to those who backed Manion because he believed it was important to support the president and let the public know where he stood.

Five Republican senators defected from party ranks and voted against Manion, while two Democrats supported him. If one more senator had voted no, Vice President Bush would not have had the opportunity to record his opinion and the controversial lawyer from Indiana would not have become an appeals court judge.

Major 5-4 Supreme Court Decisions in 1985–1986

All of these important Supreme Court cases in its 1985–1986 term were decided by a 5-4 vote.

1. In previous rulings the Supreme Court had two separate standards for judging cases involving libel. Only public officials or *public individuals* (persons well known to the general public) seeking libel damages had to prove that a statement was false and also published with "actual malice"—that is, published with prior knowledge that it was false or with reckless disregard for its truth or falsity. *Private individuals* (persons not known to the general public) could win libel suits simply by claiming that a falsehood was published with negligence. This meant that news organizations had to bear the burden of proving the truth of defamatory statements about private individuals.

In a 1986 case, however, the Supreme Court decreed that when a matter involves an issue of public concern, private individuals, as well as public figures, must prove that damaging media statements about them are false. The Court declared that the burden of proof must be borne by the plaintiff bringing the suit. Otherwise, free speech by news organizations fearful of lawsuits could be limited.

The four dissenting justices assailed the majority decision as a "blueprint for character assassination." They argued that it failed to protect private reputations from libelous accusations.

2. After a car chase and shootout, Dennis Banks and three other persons were arrested by Oregon police in 1975 for illegally transporting 350 pounds of dynamite, 6 time bombs, 2,600 rounds of ammunition, and assorted firearms. The trial of the defendants was delayed for years by pretrial appeals as the defense and prosecution argued about the defendants' attempts to suppress evidence and gain dismissal of the charges. Finally, in 1983, the district court held that the defendants' rights to a speedy trial had been denied and dismissed the charges. This ruling was upheld by the U.S. Ninth Circuit Court of Appeals.

When the case reached the Supreme Court, the justices overturned the appeals court decision. The Court ruled that the time during pretrial appeals, when defendants are neither under indictment nor otherwise restricted, may not be counted as intentional delay. Justice Lewis F. Powell, Jr., writing for the Court majority, said, "There is no showing of bad faith or dilatory purpose on the government's part. The government's position in each of the appeals was strong. . . ." The overriding significance of this 5-4 Court decision was that, under certain circumstances, the constitutional right to a speedy trial may be limited.

3. A rabbi in the Air Force frequently wore a skullcap, or yarmulke, while on duty. Wearing the skullcap was a form of religious observance common among Orthodox Jews, but it violated the dress regulations of the armed forces. When the rabbi refused to stop wearing the skullcap on duty, he was reprimanded and threatened with court-martial. Later he left the service, filed suit, and obtained a district court ruling that the Air Force had violated his rights.

This ruling was overturned by an appeals panel, so the rabbi took his case to the Supreme Court, alleging that the First Amendment protected his right to wear religious apparel in the armed forces unless it created a "clear danger." The Supreme Court, in its 5-4 decision, sided with the Air Force and declared that the constitutional right to free exercise of religion does not require the armed services to permit practices that would detract from the uniformity sought by dress regulations. "The considered professional judgment of the Air Force is that . . . standardized uniforms encourage the subordination of personal preferences and identities in favor of the overall group mission," Justice William Rehnquist wrote for the majority. ". . . Military officials are under no constitutional mandate to abandon their considered professional judgment."

4. Ten white tenured teachers in Jackson, Michigan, lost their jobs under an agreement between the school district and the teachers' union that protected blacks from layoffs even if they had less seniority than whites. The white teachers had seniority and, claiming that they were the victims of reverse discrimination, sued to be reinstated.

The Supreme Court voted 5-4 in favor of the white teachers, declaring that the school district layoff plan violated the equal protection clause of the Fourteenth Amendment. The Court said that affirmative action programs must be carefully drawn and are not acceptable merely because of a general "societal discrimination" against minorities.

This 5-4 decision, however, did not strike down all affirmative action programs. For though the Court ruled on behalf of the white teachers with seniority, most of the justices in their written opinions seemed to accept the notion that an employer could help compensate for past discrimination by race-preferential hiring goals, and need not limit that remedy to identifiable individual victims. Justice Lewis F. Powell, Jr.

wrote that "in order to remedy the effects of prior discrimination, it may be necessary to take race into account." That could mean, he added, that "innocent persons may be called upon to bear some of the burden of the remedy."

5. Less than two months after the Supreme Court had overturned the Jackson school district's layoff policy as reverse discrimination, it upheld affirmative action programs in two other situations. The Court, in a 5-4 ruling, approved of a federal court order establishing a 29 percent minority membership goal for a sheet metal workers' union in New York that had long excluded nonwhite applicants. It upheld also, by a 6-3 vote, a federal-court-approved agreement in Cleveland, Ohio, that promised minorities half of the promotions in the fire department, regardless of whether they were elevated over whites with more seniority and higher test scores.

Justice William Brennan, writing for the majority in the New York case, said, "A court may have to resort to race-conscious affirmative action when confronted with an employer or labor union that has engaged in persistent or egregious discrimination. Or such relief may be necessary to dissipate the lingering effects of pervasive discrimination."

After many years of bitter controversy over affirmative action, the Supreme Court, in its 1985-1986 term, seemed to have finally reached a consensus: Employers may give minority preference in hiring and promotions, providing whites are not directly hurt by losing the jobs they already hold.

6. Police officers in Santa Clara, California, had received an anonymous tip in 1982 that marijuana was being grown in the backyard of Dante Ciraolo. Unable to see over two tall fences that surrounded the yard, the officers chartered a plane, and from the air they spotted and photographed a large cluster of seventy-three marijuana plants. Then they obtained a search warrant, confiscated the plants, and arrested Ciraolo. After a trial court turned down his effort to suppress the evidence, Ciraolo pleaded guilty. But the California appeals court dismissed his conviction, claiming that the officers should have gotten a warrant before their air search.

The closely divided Supreme Court ruled that the police did not need search warrants to fly over fenced residential areas to search for marijuana. Chief Justice Warren Burger wrote the majority opinion for the Court, saying, "In an age where private and commercial flight in the public airways is routine, it is unreasonable for [the defendant] to expect that his marijuana plants were constitutionally protected from being observed with the naked eye from an altitude of 1,000 feet."

In a related case the Supreme Court, by the same 5-4 margin, declared that the federal Environmental Protection Agency had the authority to take aerial photographs without a warrant of the facilities of a chemical firm suspected of violating clean-air laws.

7. An Illinois woman who had been found guilty of murder argued that the use of her codefendant's out-of-court confession had violated her constitutional right to confront all adverse witnesses during trial.

Reversing lower case rulings, the Supreme Court set aside the woman's conviction, thus reinforcing an important constitutional protection—the Sixth Amendment guarantee of the right of the accused to confront and cross-examine witnesses. The high court then sent the case back to the Illinois courts to determine whether there was sufficient evidence to convict the defendant without the inadmissible confession of the codefendant.

8. In Puerto Rico gambling casinos are legal. However, a Puerto Rican law prohibited casino owners from advertising their businesses on the island, but they were permitted to run ads on the United States mainland in an attempt to draw tourists. A casino owner who was fined for breaking this law appealed his case all the way to the Supreme Court, contending that the law violated his First Amendment right of free speech.

The high court upheld the Puerto Rican law by a 5-4 vote. "The particular kind of commercial speech at issue . . . may be restricted only if the government's interest in doing so is substantial," wrote Justice William Rehnquist for the Court majority. But the Puerto Rican legislature's belief that "excessive casino gambling . . . would produce serious harmful effects on health, safety and welfare of Puerto Rican citizens . . . constitutes a 'substantial' governmental interest," he concluded.

This decision, affirming that Puerto Rico could ban ads for casinos because they allegedly had "serious harmful effects" on the health and welfare of its citizens, raised the hopes of those seeking to ban tobacco advertising in the United States.

9. In its first major case on a gay rights issue, the Supreme Court had to deal with a Georgia law making sodomy a crime. A federal appellate court had struck down the law on the grounds that it violated constitutional rights and that sexual conduct in private was beyond state regula-

tion. The high court, however, reversed this ruling and thus refused to extend the right to privacy to homosexual behavior between consenting adults.

Writing for the 5-4 majority, Justice Byron White said that prohibitions against homosexual conduct have "ancient roots" and sodomy was "forbidden by the laws of the 13 states when they ratified the Bill of Rights." White added, "To claim that a right to engage in [homosexual sodomy] is 'deeply rooted in the nation's history and tradition' . . . is, at best, facetious."

The majority of justices insisted that the Supreme Court should show "great resistance" against any effort to "discover new fundamental rights" not spelled out in the Constitution. "Otherwise," Justice White declared in opposition to an activist Court, "the judiciary necessarily takes to itself further authority to govern the country without express constitutional authority."

In a bristling dissent to the Court's decision on policing homosexual behavior, Justice Harry Blackmun wrote, "Depriving individuals of the right to choose for themselves how to conduct their intimate relationships poses a far greater threat to the values most deeply rooted in our nation's history than tolerance of nonconformity could ever do."

10. Few issues have divided the nation as sharply in recent years as *Roe* v. *Wade*, the 1973 Supreme Court decision protecting women's constitutional right to abortion. In 1986, the Court ruled again on an abortion issue. This time the Court had to deal with a Pennsylvania law designed to discourage women from having abortions.

The Pennsylvania law, which was passed in 1982, required physicians to tell pregnant patients considering abortion about possible detrimental physical and psychological effects of abortion and to provide information about agencies available to help them if they decided to give birth. The law also forced doctors to record intimate details about a woman seeking an abortion, file certain data for public record, and describe to her the characteristics of the fetus at two-week intervals.

The Supreme Court, in a 5-4 decision, struck down the Pennsylvania law. Expressing the opinion of the majority, Justice Harry Blackmun wrote, "The states are not free, under the guise of protecting maternal health or potential life, to intimidate women into continuing pregnancies." Close analysis of the provisions of the Pennsylvania law, Blackmun continued, "shows that they wholly subordinate constitutional privacy interests and concerns with maternal health in an effort to deter a woman from making a decision that, with her physician, is hers to make. . . ."

The four dissenting justices took issue not only with the majority opinion but also with the landmark *Roe* v. *Wade* decision thirteen years earlier. Chief Justice Warren Burger called the ruling in the Pennsylvania case "astonishing" and suggested that *Roe* v. *Wade* (which he had supported in 1973) should be "reexamined." In another dissent, Justice Byron White, joined by Justice William Rehnquist, described the 1973 decision as "fundamentally misguided" and urged that it be overturned. Justice Sandra Day O'Connor echoed this philosophy when she said that *Roe* v. *Wade* had proved "unworkable."

Both sides of the abortion issue found something to cheer about in the Court ruling on the Pennsylvania law. Those who believed in free choice for women were delighted that the majority of justices still agreed with this principle. Those who opposed abortion were pleased that the proabortion vote of 7 to 2 in *Roe* v. *Wade* had shrunk to 5 to 4 in the Pennsylvania case. They surmised that the day might come soon when the justices against abortion would have the one additional vote to constitute a majority on the Supreme Court.

Epilogue

A tie-breaking run has put baseball teams into the World Series. A free throw at the buzzer has sent basketball teams to the NCAA finals. A kicked conversion has earned football teams the chance to play in a bowl game. One-point victories, common in the world of sports, are always suspenseful and usually exciting.

One-vote decisions in the realm of politics also are suspenseful and can be exciting. Moreover, a one-vote decision may have important, far-reaching ramifications. It can elect a candidate and impeach a government official. It can pass or defeat a bill in the legislature and cause the success or failure of a ballot measure. It can determine the fate of an issue before the Supreme Court. It can confirm or deny the appointment of a person nominated for a government position. It can ratify or reject a treaty. It can approve or strike down a constitutional amendment and even decide whether another constitutional convention will be called.

These crucial one-vote decisions occur much more often than most people realize.

Further Reading

Ambrose, Stephen E. *Eisenhower*. New York: Simon and Schuster, 1983.
Bailey, Thomas A. *A Diplomatic History of the American People*. New York: F. S. Crofts, 1946.
Bartholomew, Paul C., and Joseph F. Menez. *Summaries of Leading Cases on the Constitution*. Totowa, N.J.: Rowman and Allanheld, 1983.
Bartlett, Ruhl J., ed. *The Record of American Diplomacy*. New York: Knopf, 1947.
Bates, Ernest S. *The Story of Congress, 1789-1935*. New York: Harper, 1936.
Boller, Paul F., Jr. *Presidential Campaigns*. New York: Oxford University Press, 1984.
Burns, James MacGregor. *The Workshop of Democracy*. New York: Knopf, 1985.
Castel, Albert. *The Yeas and the Nays: Key Congressional Decisions, 1774-1945*. Kalamazoo, Mich.: New Issues Press, 1975.
Chalmers, David M. *Hooded Americanism: The First Century of the Ku Klux Klan, 1865-1965*. Garden City, N.Y.: Doubleday, 1965.
Congressional Quarterly Inc. *The Supreme Court and Individual Rights*. Washington: Congressional Quarterly Inc., 1980.
Corbin, Carole L. *The Right to Vote*. New York: Watts, 1985.
Devine, Robert A. *Eisenhower and the Cold War*. New York: Oxford University Press, 1981.
Flexner, Eleanor. *Century of Struggle: The Woman's Rights Movement in the United States*. Cambridge: Harvard University Press, 1959.
Fribourg, Marjorie G. *The U.S. Congress: Men Who Steered Its Course, 1787-1867*. Philadelphia: M. Smith Co., 1972.
Friendly, Fred W., and Martha J. H. Elliott. *The Constitution: That Delicate Balance*. New York: Random House, 1984.
Gallagher, Hugh G. *Advise and Obstruct: The Role of the United States Senate in Foreign Policy Decisions*. New York: Delacorte Press, 1969.
Galloway, George B. *History of the House of Representatives*. New York: Crowell, 1976.
Garrison, Webb. *Behind the Headlines: American History's Schemes, Scandals and Escapades*. Harrisburg, Pa.: Stackpole Books, 1983.

124 / Further Reading

Gerson, Noel B. *The Slender Reed: A Biographical Novel of James Knox Polk.* Garden City, N.Y.: Doubleday, 1965.

Goode, Stephen. *The Controversial Court: Supreme Court Influences on American Life.* New York: Messner, 1982.

Haynes, George. *The Senate of the United States: Its History and Practice,* 2 vols. Boston: Houghton Mifflin, 1938.

Hentoff, Nat. *The First Freedom: The Tumultuous History of Free Speech in America.* New York: Dell, 1981.

Josephy, Alvin M. *On the Hill: A History of the American Congress.* New York: Simon and Schuster, 1979.

Kennedy, John F. *Profiles in Courage.* New York: Harper and Row, 1961.

Lindop, Edmund, and Joy Crane Thornton. *All about Democrats.* Hillside, N.J.: Enslow, 1985.

Lindop, Edmund. *All about Republicans.* Hillside, N.J.: Enslow, 1985.

———. *Birth of the Constitution.* Hillside, N.J.: Enslow, 1987.

Lyon, Peter. *Eisenhower: Portrait of the Hero.* Boston: Little, Brown, 1974.

Manchester, William. *The Glory and the Dream: A Narrative History of America, 1932-1972,* 2 vols. Boston: Little, Brown, 1974.

Mendelson, Wallace. *The Constitution and the Supreme Court.* New York: Dodd, Mead, 1965.

Mitchell, William C. *Why Vote?* Chicago: Markham, 1971.

Morgan, Ted. *FDR: A Biography.* New York: Simon and Schuster, 1985.

Padover, Saul K., and Jacob W. Landynski. *The Living U.S. Constitution.* New York: New American Library, 1983.

Pierce, Noel. *The People's President.* New York: Simon and Schuster, 1968.

Roseboom, Eugene H., and Alfred E. Eckles, Jr. *A History of Presidential Elections from George Washington to Jimmy Carter,* 4th ed. New York: Macmillan, 1979.

Schapsmeier, Edward L. *Dirksen of Illinois: Senatorial Statesman.* Urbana: University of Illinois Press, 1985.

Severn, Bill. *The Right to Vote.* New York: Ives Washburn, 1972.

Smith, Page. *The Constitution: A Documentary and Narrative History.* New York: Morrow, 1978.

Starr, Isidore. *The Idea of Liberty: First Amendment Freedoms.* St. Paul, Minn.: West, 1978.

Switzer, Ellen E. *There Ought to Be a Law: How Laws Are Made and Work.* New York: Atheneum, 1972.

Index

Abortion, 121–22
Adams, John, 14–15, 18, 20, 23, 29
Adams, John Quincy, 24, 26–32
Affirmative action, 112–14, 118–19
Agnew, Spiro T., 36
Agricultural Adjustment Act, 87–88
Alabama, 39, 44, 79
Alaska, 104
Ames, Fisher, 22–23
Arizona, 74, 97, 104
Articles of Confederation, 11, 13

Baker v. Carr, 99–100
Bakke, Allan, 113–14
Barnhart, Henry, 76
Barnum, William, 61
Bayh, Birch, 104
Bedford, Gunning, Jr., 12
Benton, Thomas Hart, 36, 71
Bill of Rights, 54–56, 83, 101, 106, 109, 111, 121
Bingham, John A., 54
Birney, James G., 41
Black, Hugo, 105
Black Codes, 48
Blackmun, Harry, 107, 114, 121
Blaine, James G., 58–60
Bradley, Joseph P., 55, 64
Branch v. Texas, 107
Brandeis, Louis D., 86
Brennan, William, 107, 109–11, 114, 119
Bricker, John W., 92–94
Bricker Amendment, 92–95
Bryan, William Jennings, 80
Buchanan, James, 60

Burger, Warren E., 98–99, 107, 111, 113, 119, 122
Burke, Edward R., 90
Bush, George, 116
Butler, Pierce, 84, 86
Byrd, Robert C., 116

Calhoun, John C., 26, 29–36
Calhoun, Mrs. John C., 33
California, 41, 74, 79, 96, 110, 116, 119
Capital punishment, 106–8
Cardozo, Benjamin N., 86
Cass, Lewis, 34, 40
Chandler, Zachariah, 61
Chase, Salmon P., 52
Chicago Tribune, 83, 92
Chinn, Julia, 38
Cincinnati Enquirer, 65
Ciraolo, Dante, 119
Civil Rights Act of 1866, 49–50
Civil Rights Act of 1964, 112, 115
Civil War, 30, 44, 47, 58–60, 66, 71
Clay, Henry, 25–29, 35–36, 40–41, 43, 71
Colorado, 74, 79
Compromise of 1877, 66
Connecticut, 12–13, 61, 72, 96–97
Constitution, U.S., 11–14, 21, 50, 54, 63, 65, 66–67, 72, 83, 93, 98, 100–101, 103, 106, 111
Constitutional Amendments: First, 83–84, 109–11, 118, 120; Fifth, 96–98; Sixth, 97, 120; Eighth, 106–7; Twelfth, 27; Thirteenth, 48; Fourteenth, 49–51, 54–56, 84, 99, 101, 107, 118; Fifteenth, 51, 74; Sixteenth, 67–68; Seventeenth,

125

126 / Index

70–72; Nineteenth, 73–77; Twenty-sixth, 102–6
Constitutional Convention, 1787, 11–13
Coolidge, Calvin, 78, 81–83
"Corrupt Bargain," 29
Cranston, Alan, 116
Crawford, William H., 25–28, 33
Crosser, Robert, 76

Dallas, George M., 41–42
Daugherty, Harry M., 78
Davis, David, 63–64
Davis, John W., 81
Dawes, Charles G., 82
Dayton, Jonathan, 23
DeFunis v. *Odegaard*, 112–13
Delaware, 11–13, 28, 52
Democratic party, 34, 37–46, 49, 53, 58–66, 71, 78–81, 87, 92, 116
Dickinson, John, 11
Dirksen, Everett M., 100–102
Dirksen Amendment, 100–102
Dole, Robert, 116
Donelson, Mrs. Andrew, 33
Douglas, William O., 100, 107, 111
Dulles, John Foster, 93–94

Eaton, John H., 33–34
Eaton, Peggy O'Neale, 33–35
Eisenhower, Dwight D., 92–96, 103
Elections, presidential: 1820, 24; 1824, 25–29; 1828, 29, 32; 1832, 34–36; 1836, 36–39; 1840, 39; 1844, 40–41; 1864, 46; 1868, 52; 1872, 58; 1876, 58–66; 1920, 78; 1924, 78–81; 1936, 87; 1952, 92; 1984, 9–10
Electoral College, 24, 27–29, 50
Ellsberg, Daniel, 85
Escobedo v. *Illinois*, 97–98

Fall, Albert B., 78
Federalist party, 17–20, 22, 24
Field, Stephen J., 56
Florida, 58, 61–64
Franklin, Benjamin, 12, 102
Frazier-Lemke Act, 87–88
Frelinghuysen, Frederick T., 64
Fuller, Melville W., 67
Furman v. *Georgia*, 107

Gallatin, Albert, 22
George, Walter, 95
George Amendment, 95
Georgia, 12–13, 20, 25, 46, 95, 103–5, 108, 120
Gideon v. *Wainwright*, 97

Ginzburg v. *United States*, 110
Gitlow v. *New York*, 56
Goldberg, Arthur J., 97
Goldwater, Barry, 104
Granger, Francis, 39
Grant, Ulysses S., 44, 51–52, 57–58, 62, 65
Great Britain, 15–22, 35, 41–42, 83, 89–91, 102
Greeley, Horace, 58
Gregg v. *Georgia*, 108
Grimes, James W., 53
Guffey-Snyder Coal Conservation Act, 87

Hamilton, Alexander, 12, 17–18, 20
Hammond, George, 18
Hanna, Mark, 68
Harding, Warren G., 78
Harlan, John Marshall, 67
Harriman, Edward H., 68–69
Harrison, William Henry, 37, 39–40
Hatch, Orrin G., 116
Hawaii, 104
Hayes, Rutherford B., 59–66
Hicks, Frederick, 76
Hill, James J., 68–69
Hitler, Adolf, 89–91
Hodgkinson, John, 17
Holmes, Oliver Wendell, 70
Hughes, Charles E., 83–86, 88–89

Idaho, 74
Illinois, 28, 54, 76, 97, 100–101
Income tax, 66–68
Independent Treasury System, 41–42
Indiana, 61, 76, 104, 115–16
Ingersoll, Robert G., 59–60
Iowa, 53, 101

Jackson, Andrew, 26–29, 31–38
Jackson, Rachel, 33
Jackson v. *Georgia*, 107
Jay, John, 18–22
Jay Treaty, 18–23
Jefferson, Thomas, 17, 20, 25, 32, 37
Johnson, Andrew, 14–15, 43–54
Johnson, Eliza McCardle, 44
Johnson, Forney, 79
Johnson, Lyndon B., 95, 112
Johnson, Richard M., 37–39

Kansas, 74, 116
Kennedy, Edward, 104
Kentucky, 20, 28, 37–39, 104–5, 115
Knowland, William, 94–95

Index / 127

Knox, Philander C., 69
Korean War, 103
Ku Klux Klan, 57, 79–81

LaFollette, Robert M., 81
Lee, Robert E., 44
Lend-Lease Act, 91
Lewis, John L., 90
Liberal Republican party, 58
Liberty party, 41
Lincoln, Abraham, 43–47, 51–52, 65
Lindbergh, Charles A., 89
Lippmann, Walter, 94
Livingston, Edward, 22
Louisiana, 28, 44, 55, 57, 58, 61–64, 108

McAdoo, William Gibbs, 79, 81
MacArthur, Douglas, 101
McCarthy, Joseph, 93
McClellan, George B., 46
McDonald, Larry P., 115
McGautha v. *California*, 107
McKinley, William, 68
McLane, Louis, 28–29
McReynolds, James C., 86
Madison, James, 14, 17, 22, 25, 37, 102
Maine, 58, 72
Malloy v. *Hogan*, 96–97
Manion, Clarence, 115
Manion, Daniel A., 115–16
Mann, James, 76
Mansfield, Mike, 95, 104
Marshall, George C., 91
Marshall, John, 96
Marshall, Thurgood, 107, 114
Martin, Luther, 11
Maryland, 11, 13, 28
Massachusetts, 11, 13, 16, 20, 26, 49, 104
Michigan, 40, 81, 83, 118
Military Reconstruction Act, 50
Miller v. *California*, 110
Minnesota, 83–85, 114
Miranda v. *Arizona*, 97–99
Mississippi, 45, 48
Missouri, 28, 74, 79
Monroe, James, 24–25
Montana, 90
Moore, Gabriel, 36
Morgan, J. P., 69
Morris, Gouverneur, 12–13
Morse, Samuel, 41
Muhlenberg, Frederick, 23
Murray, James, 90

National Labor Relations Act, 88
National Recovery Act, 86–87

Near v. *Minnesota*, 83–85
Nebraska, 90
New Deal, 86–89
New Hampshire, 17, 26, 28, 31
New Jersey, 12–13, 43, 61, 64
New York, 13, 17, 20, 25, 27–29, 34, 39, 41, 58, 61, 68, 76, 79, 87, 90, 105, 119
New York Times, 61, 85, 93
Niles, Hezekiah, 25
Niles' Weekly Register, 25
Nixon, Richard M., 98, 104–5
North Carolina, 13, 44, 108
Northern Securities Company, 68–70
Nullification doctrine, 31–32

Obscenity, 109–11
O'Connor, Sandra Day, 122
Ohio, 28, 59, 76, 78, 90, 92, 108, 119
Oklahoma, 81
Oregon, 63–64, 72, 74, 105
Oregon Territory, 41–42

Paterson, William, 12
Peace Treaty of 1783, 15
Pennington, William, 43
Pennsylvania, 11–13, 23, 41–42, 45, 121–22
Pentagon Papers, 85
Pinckney, Charles Cotesworth, 13
Pitt, William, 17
Plumer, William, 24
Polk, James K., 40–42
Pollock v. *Farmers' Loan and Trust Company*, 67
Populist party, 71
Powell, Lewis, F., Jr., 107, 114, 117–18
Progressive party, 81
Prohibition, 79
Proxmire, William, 101
Puerto Rico, 120

Radical Republicans, 47–54, 56–66, 82
Railroad Retirement Act, 86
Randolph, Jennings, 103
Randolph, John, 30
Rayburn, Sam, 91
Reagan, Ronald, 99, 115
Reconstruction Acts of 1867, 51
Reconstruction period, 46–66, 72
Rehnquist, William, 99, 107, 113, 118, 120, 122
Reid, John C., 61
Republican party, 43–54, 56–66, 78–81, 92, 94, 96, 116
Republican party (Democratic-Republican), 17–25, 37

128 / Index

Revolutionary War, 16, 19
Rhode Island, 12
Roberts, Owen J., 86, 88–89
Robson, George M., 64
Roe v. *Wade*, 121–22
Roosevelt, Eleanor, 93
Roosevelt, Franklin D., 79–80, 86–93, 105
Roosevelt, Theodore, 68–70, 86
Roth v. *United States*, 109
Russell, Richard, 103

Sargent, John G., 83
Saturday Press, 84
Scalia, Antonin, 99
Seminole War, 26–27, 32, 38
Seneca Falls Convention, 73
Sheridan, Philip K., 46
Sherman, James S., 72–73
Sherman, Roger, 12–13
Sherman, William T., 46, 62
Sherman Antitrust Act, 69–70
Sims, Thetus, 75–76
Slaughterhouse Cases, 55–56
Slavery, 26, 44, 46
Smith, Alfred E., 79–81
Smith, Margaret Chase, 95
Smith, William, 39
Social Security Act, 86, 88
South Carolina, 13, 17, 20, 26, 30–31, 58, 60–64, 74
Spanish Florida, 26, 28, 33
Springer v. *United States*, 66
Stalin, Josef, 92
Stanbery, Henry, 82
Stanton, Edwin M., 51–52
Stanton, Elizabeth Cady, 73, 77
Stephens, Alexander, 48–49
Stevens, John G., 64
Stevens, John Paul, 113–14
Stevens, Thaddeus, 49, 52
Stewart, Potter, 107–9, 113
Stone, Harlan F., 86
Sumner, Charles, 49
Sutherland, George, 86
Swayne, Noah, 55–56
Sweeney, Martin L., 90

Taft, William Howard, 70
Taney, Roger B., 34
Tariff: of 1816, 30; of 1827, 30; of 1828, 31; of 1842, 41; Walker, 42
Tecumseh, 37–38
Tennessee, 36, 39–40, 44–45, 51, 54, 76–77, 99

Tenure of Office Act, 14–15, 51–53
Texas, 40–41, 105
Thomas, Lorenzo, 52
Tilden, Samuel J., 60–66
Tillman, Ben, 74
Truman, Harry, 92–93
Trumbull, Lyman, 54
Tweed, William (Boss), 58, 60
Tyler, John, 39–41

Underwood, Oscar W., 79
Union party, 46
University of California Regents v. *Bakke*, 113–14
Utah, 74, 116

Van Buren, Martin, 34–41
Van Devanter, Willis, 86
Van Rensselaer, Stephen, 28–29
Vermont, 20, 83
Vest, George, 74
Vietnam War, 85, 104
Virginia, 11, 13–14, 24, 30, 38–40
Voting age, 102–6
Voting Rights Act of 1970, 104–5

Wade-Davis Bill, 47
Wadsworth, James W., 90
Wadsworth-Burke Act, 90
Walker, Robert J., 42
Warren, Charles B., 81–83
Warren, Earl, 96, 98
Warren Court, 96–102, 107
Washington (state), 74
Washington, George, 14–15, 17–22, 24–25, 102
Washington Post, 85, 93
Webster, Daniel, 28, 35–36, 39–40, 71
West Indies, 16, 19
West Virginia, 103
Wheeler, Burton K., 90–91
Whig party, 37–43
White, Byron R., 97–98, 107, 114, 121–22
White, Hugh L., 39
Whitney, Eli, 19
Willkie, Wendell, 90
Wilson, James, 11
Wilson, Woodrow, 74–77, 79, 81
Wisconsin, 81, 101
Women's suffrage, 73–77
World War I, 75–76
World War II, 89–91, 103
Wright, Silas, 41
Wyoming, 74